YOUR MOVE

YOUR MOVE

YOUR MOVE

The Underdog's Guide to Building Your Business

Ramit Sethi

First publication June 2017

ISBN-10: 0692940081

ISBN-13: 9780692940082

HOW TO USE THIS BOOK

Two quick notes:

I wrote this book for busy people.

Each chapter can be read as a stand-alone resource. So while you'll get the most out of the book reading each chapter in order, feel free to jump around to find the lessons you need, as you need them.

I also wrote this book to be *timeless*.

One of the biggest weaknesses of business books is that authors fill them with tactics that simply stop working as the market changes. After a few months, or maybe a few years, the book becomes totally useless.

That's why I focused this book on the psychological mindsets and fundamental business principles every entrepreneur needs to be successful.

But I want to make sure you still have access to the most effective, up-to date marketing tactics and business strategies.

So I set up a members only website for this book that my team and I can easily keep up to date.

Lifetime access is included with your purchase. All you have to do to claim it is go to the website below.

www.growthlab.com/your-move

Here are just a few of the resources we've included. (Note that these may change over time as certain tactics stop working and others are developed.)

- Instant Authority: How to quickly establish your credibility in any market
- GrowthLab Insider: How to build a $100,000 business in 12 months
- Word-for-word negotiating scripts used by some of the world's top freelancers
- Notes from a $25,000 private strategy session—discover the exact advice I gave a good friend as they started their own business
- And more…

Enjoy the book, and thanks for reading.

– Ramit Sethi

TABLE OF CONTENTS

PRAISE FOR RAMIT SETHI

What people are saying about Ramit Sethi

"Ramit Sethi is on the short list of people I respect in the world of finance. Ramit built his personal finance blog up to more than 1 million+ readers per month, and has turned it into a revenue generating monster and a growing business..."—Tim Ferriss, fourhourworkweek.com

"He is Generation Y's favorite personal finance adviser. His message: Motivation isn't enough. Develop a system, and get over yourself."—Fortune

"Ramit is a trainer. He'll make you hustle."—James Altucher

What Ramit's Students Are Saying

"I went from no business, no idea—nothing—to having my first launch in 3 months. With only an email list of 340 people, I made $1,749 in 3 days. [Ramit's work] changed my life."— Alice Bush, aliceslifestyle.com

"It's been amazing...Recently I had a launch that earned me over $10,000."—William Horvath, permacultureapprentice.com

"It's a year since I started...and I can't believe where I am now compared to where I was then. My revenue doubles every time I launch a course or a product."—Amy Shah, amyshahmd.com

"I never saw myself as an entrepreneurial person...[Ramit's work] gave me the roadmap to lay the foundation."—Caitlin Skidmore, greaterthanrubies.net

"The freedom is incredible...I was driving to New York and spent the entire day in the car. When I got to the hotel, I realized I made 5 sales while we were driving. That's $1,500 in revenue."—Danny Margulies, freelancetowin.com

"When I look at why I've been successful, it's because I followed Ramit's systems."—Selena Soo, selenasoo.com

"In a 24-hour period I booked $67,000 worth of work."—Daren Smith, darentsmith.com

"I know I can replace my 9-5 job...because I have a clear roadmap to go from where I am now to where I want to be."—Alison Hummel, alisonhummel.com

"Before this, I barely had the confidence to call myself a business owner...Now, in just 5 months, I made $30,000. I finally consider this a real business."—Heidi Marie, sewheidi.com

"Ramit was so specific about everything from validating your idea, to the exact words you can use to pitch your first 3 paying clients. Everything worked for me... I focused on the few things that produced the biggest results. In the first 10 months of 2016, I made $86,800. That's almost 5 times what I made with my first attempt at business. And I did it in less than half the time."—Larry Lee, larrylawlaw.com

IT'S ALWAYS YOUR MOVE

Do we need another book promising overnight success and piles of cash?

Let me be the first to tell you "no." In fact, *hell no*.

Like you, I've read all the endless promises of quick results. I've spent thousands of dollars on programs, courses, even in-person conferences. Some were very good. Others...not so much.

I've noticed that many books pick a single idea and spend hundreds of pages on it—webinars! Pinterest!—when really, that's just a minuscule part of a successful business.

What I *haven't* seen is a gritty guide that takes you through the process of starting a business and shows you the warts, the mistakes, and the things other people won't talk about:

- The psychology of getting unstuck
- Finding a profitable idea
- How to sell without being sleazy
- Systems for building automatic revenue
- Finding a mentor to help you grow

I know, I know. These aren't as sexy as "5 webinar strategies that will crush the competition," but they're the real topics that will help you start and grow a business.

I know, because they helped me create a business that's helped millions of people over the last 13 years, generating many millions of dollars, 800,000+ subscribers around the world, and press coverage on NBC's "Today" show, a 6-page profile in Fortune, and a photo in Forbes next to Warren Buffett.

I have to be candid: If you're reading this book and hoping someone will give you a magical idea that will give you millions, you should just put it down. Or if you're looking for someone to coddle you for how busy you are, how you don't have any time, and how tough it is…I have to say, that's not me.

In fact, one of the chapters in this book is called, "Getting stuck is normal, but winners grow anyway."

In other words, yes! Life is tough! But I want to show you how to win anyway—especially if you're the "underdog."

I don't know about you, but I crave the honest truth. I want someone to tell me if I'm on the right track, to push me, and to call me on my BS.

That's why I've put together this book for you.

If you think about it, what would a business mean for you? What would it mean to be able to earn an extra $1,000 per month, or $5,000…or even $25,000 every month?

I ask a lot of people this question. They tell me they could pay down their student loans (that's a very sensible answer). But when I press them, their eyes start to shine with possibilities they never really thought about before.

"I could hire a babysitter so I could go on a date with my husband every single week."

"I could buy a round of drinks for my friends every Friday without worrying about how much it costs."

"I could take a trip to Spain and pay for my parents to come along."

I love these answers. They're specific, they're detailed, and most importantly, they're your definition of a Rich Life.

A successful business is about more than money. It's about more success, more peace of mind, more time for friends and family.

For me, my "more" is impact. I want to reach as many people as possible, which is why I published this book.

(In fact, I could reach more people by giving this away for free. So why did I charge for this? It's not the money, which is inconsequential to me. There are two reasons—the first two lessons of this book:

1. **People value what they pay for.** If I gave you this book for free, you might be excited for 5 pages, but most people wouldn't make it past that. But if you pay, you'll use it.
2. **There's a 1,000-fold difference between a free reader and a paying customer.** I'm not exaggerating—in our business, previous customers purchase

2,000 times more than first-time buyers. In other words, it's better to have a small group of committed people than a large group of random readers!)

Back to what a business can mean for you. More—more success, more time, more money—doesn't have to mean pure extravagance. Although it's totally fine if that's what you want. More success can be simple things. For example, I absolutely love going to a restaurant and ordering whatever I want. (Growing up, my family only went out when we had coupons and never ordered appetizers, so this is a massive luxury for me.)

If you're just starting out, an extra $1,000 a month can dramatically improve your quality of life. Fortunately, there's a TON of ways to earn an extra $1,000. In fact, when you break down the numbers, it's not very hard:

- $1,000/month = $250/week
- $250/week = $50/day, 5 days a week

So you just need to earn an extra $50, Monday through Friday.

That's achievable. And the beauty of it?

Now here's your third lesson:

It's not magic. It's math.

By the end of this book, you'll know that a profitable business is not some magical thing that only certain people can do. It's straightforward and you can do it, too. You don't need to know advanced calculus to run a business, but I find it comforting to know that I can "break down" the math of a $10,000 business, or $100,000, or even $1 million or $10 million.

So, how can you earn that extra $1,000 this month? You can freelance. Find jobs on Craigslist. You can cut back on spending money on things you don't want or use. You can flip items on eBay. You can find a better job, or negotiate a higher salary at your current one. I've taught tens of thousands of students how to do all of these.

Any of these could work. However, in my opinion, the best way to earn extra money by far is starting your own business. Why? Because with things like salary negotiations and selling on eBay, there's a natural ceiling you're going to hit. For example, even if you're the world's best negotiator, there's only so much a company can pay you.

But when you start your own business, there's no limit to how much you can earn.

And that's what you're going to learn in this book: How to start, run, and grow your business.

> "I have all these ideas. I like giving people advice. I never really thought that I could make money out of it…And [now] I've had months where I've made close to the amount that I made in an entire year working a non-profit."—Selena S.

> "You can always make more money. It takes hard work and a good strong system and support behind you. It's fun now, being able to continue doing the hobbies that I love without having to say, 'I have to drop something because I can't afford it.'"—Doug F.

It's Not Magic, It's Math

You already know you can make $1,000 extra. If you can make $1,000, you can make $10,000 (which is over $100,000 a year). With that kind of money, you can double your income, quit your 9-5, or give it all away. The point is, you have options.

Believe it or not, if you can make $100,000, then it's possible to reach $1,000,000.

I know it sounds farfetched at first. "Are you saying if I read this book, Ramit, you'll turn me into a millionaire in a few weeks?!" No. Candidly, most people reading this will not become millionaires because it involves extremely hard work and insane perseverance.

Anyone who promises you a million bucks is lying.

But I can also tell you I've created many millionaires.

And many of my readers are generating hundreds of thousands of dollars a year following the steps I gave them. Not just 1 or 2 people, but a lot.

So: If you put in the work (which took me YEARS), find a business idea people want to pay for, and can already make $100,000, it's possible to implement the right systems so that revenue eventually grows to $1,000,000. I never thought my blog would generate over $1,000,000...until it did. And then much more.

Funny story: The first time it happened, I didn't even know. One of my team members emailed me in the middle of the night:

From: M████ ████████ ████████
Date: Tue, ████████████ at 12:46 AM
Subject: Epic win...congrats dude.
To: Ramit Sethi <ramit@ramitsethi.com>

You hit a million bucks! Did you know that?

Again, it's not magic, it's just math. Here's what $1,000,000 in revenue looks like:

- $50 product x 20,000 sales
- $100 product x 10,000 sales
- $200 product x 5,000 sales
- $500 product x 2,000 sales
- $1,000 product x 1,000 sales

For the 5,000 people about to email me that I didn't include taxes, FICA, refunds, and more—I know. This is a model. The point is to show you that generating $1 million is not some mythical, unattainable goal that you can never get. You use models to see the possibilities, then you go deeper to make it happen.

Why Not You?

Once I started delving into this, I started to understand how business really works, and I realized we're standing at the greatest opportunity in our lifetimes. For the first time, we don't have to wait for some gatekeeper in Manhattan or at some fancy company to choose us and give us a shot.

We don't have to toil for 30 years, chasing a meaningless credential or kissing up to the right person, and wait for a lucky day. We can actually create our own luck.

By the way, you can do a fraction of this and completely change the trajectory of your life. That's happened with thousands of my students:

> *"I checked my email and voila! I had made a sale and was richer by $700! I can actually…hang out in the sun with my friend and still be making money!"*—Maria B.

> *"It feels like I'm almost cheating. I went to the gym…Somewhere within that timeframe, I made $100. I was not present for it. I did not sit at a desk. I did not travel. And I made money. What?! This seems unreal."*—Ben W.

> *"This past July, we just had our first child, and I was able to spend that entire month of July at her family's cottage, and all I really had to do was go check my email at the local library every three or four days to make sure that everyone was getting their online products that they were ordering okay. And I didn't have to do an hour of work."*—James A.

I've been teaching people how to save more, earn more, and live a richer life for over 10 years. They've come from all sorts of backgrounds and skillsets: dating coaches, caricaturists, violinists, PR experts, dancers, lawyers, the list goes on and on. Some of these students had no idea for their business. Others had too many and didn't know which one to pick.

I point this out so you understand: Someone's going to do it. Why should it be someone else? Why shouldn't it be you?

Because you don't have an idea? I'll show you how to find one in Chapter 2. Hate the idea of selling? We'll help you get past those fears in Chapter 6. Or, maybe you just think starting a business is too risky?

I'm not saying there aren't inherent risks to starting a business. Of course there are—that's why for most of my students, I encourage them to start it on the side, while they're still working their regular job. That's what most do, putting in 5 hours, 10 hours, sometimes more, into their business while working the 9-5. And once they're CONFIDENT their businesses can replace their income, then they quit.

You see, it seems counterintuitive, but like most entrepreneurs, I want to remove as much risk as I can from the situation. As much as possible, I want to put my money behind a sure thing. Interestingly enough, a lot of lip service is paid to the risk of starting a business. But no one talks about the invisible risk of doing nothing.

The Invisible Risk of Doing Nothing
It's funny the way we think about risk.

We look both ways before we cross the street because we know how dangerous fast cars can be. We also pay attention to a wet floor because we don't want to slip and injure ourselves. Both are very smart moves.

But sometimes, our minds don't handle the risk correctly. Take money, for example. How many people do you know who are afraid of investing in the stock market because they're worried about losing money?

What those people don't realize is they're losing money every single day, thanks to inflation. They never took even a single weekend to read a good book about personal finance, so they don't understand that by not investing, they will absolutely, positively run out of money.

Their "risk calculus" is wrong.

Same thing with failure.

No one likes to talk about failure.

But the biggest failures aren't things you did. They're things you didn't do. Playing it safe is one of the biggest failures possible. The first step is learning to recognize it in every facet of our lives.

The invisible risk of relationships means it's easy to turn down that invitation to go out on the weekend, or that blind date... until you stop getting texts on Friday and your friends settle down, leaving you eating Ben & Jerry's alone and watching bad sci-fi and romantic comedies for the rest of your life.

The invisible risk of working at a job you don't love is every day you're not being challenged, you're not just stagnant—you're actually going backwards compared to other people who are learning new skills, getting more responsibility, and getting paid what they deserve.

The invisible risk of bad health means we don't worry about that piece of cheesecake—"It's just one, right?"—but over time, we look in the mirror and see a belly and love handles. Something we vowed wouldn't happen to us.

And the invisible risk of not starting a business is that the people who wait to find "the perfect idea" get passed up by people who've started profitable businesses. The longer you wait, the more demoralizing it is to see other people soar—and the harder it gets.

The truth is you don't have to do anything about any of these things. What's the worst that could happen?

On a given day, nothing. Over a year, maybe a little. Over 10 years, the invisible risks of playing it safe add up, compound, and soon become as inescapable as a black hole.

It's not just the weight, or debt, or drudgery of marching to a job we don't love. It's the identity we create of someone who's accepted the way things are. It's as if we got on the wrong highway 500 miles ago, just realized we're going the wrong direction, and we shake our head and shrug, realizing "I guess this is where I'm going."

A Business School Compression Course

If you're reading this book, I'm pretty sure that means you understand the invisible risk of doing nothing. And you're ready to learn the business concepts that I used to build my college blog into a successful business…and how thousands of my students did too (you'll hear from them throughout this book).

Primarily, I teach business through private events and online courses. Certain events involve flying to New York City, putting yourself up in a hotel, and spending a few concentrated days with me and other students. In the online courses, my students have the luxury of taking the information and implementing it from the comfort of their own home, at their leisure. Both are amazing options that cover business building in incredible granular detail if you're ready to invest serious time and money in your business.

But eventually, I realized perhaps not everyone wants to fly to New York to learn this stuff. Or maybe they don't have the time to sit through an intensive, 8-week course.

That's why I put together this book. This is a distillation of my 10+ years building businesses, where I've created 20+ products and written over 1,000 free articles for my students. Think of it as a "compression course": The 80/20 core lessons and skills that allow me and thousands of students to live rich lives.

Inside this book, you'll find the building blocks of how to start, run, and grow your business. I'll even introduce you to a few students who used these exact same lessons to build their own 6-figure businesses. And because my bread and butter has always been crunchy tactics, like the exact words to say to negotiate your salary, I've included those as well (like how to know if your business idea has demand AND will be profitable).

Building a business isn't rocket science. But it takes you putting aside those barriers in your head—the one telling you, "You can't do this...you don't have an idea...you're not an 'entrepreneur'...why would anybody listen to you...you know NOTHING about business!"

So before you dive into this book, I want you to promise me one thing: For the next few days, or week, or however long it takes to read this book, I want you to turn off that part of your brain. Just put it on pause—not forever, just while you're reading. I want you to go into this with a beginner's mind—thinking that anything is possible.

If you can do that, when you come out the other side, you'll know it's true.

PART 1: MASTERING THE FUNDAMENTALS

My favorite is when people email me and say, "Ramit, I think I'm too advanced for your course. Got anything more advanced?"

I already know what's coming when I email them back.

Me: "Oh, interesting. How much revenue is your business generating?"

Cocky guy: "Well, I made $12.62 last month. My site is really growing."

It takes me a few minutes to respond since I have to wait for my fist to uncurl so I can type back.

What I WANT to say is: "THE MATERIAL IN THIS COURSE GENERATED MILLIONS AND MILLIONS OF DOLLARS AND TENS OF THOUSANDS OF CUSTOMERS WHO LOVE US. WHAT KIND OF PERSON THINKS THEIR BUSINESS IS TOO ADVANCED WHEN THEY ONLY GENERATE ENOUGH REVENUE TO BUY A SUBWAY SANDWICH?"

You can't help people who are too smart for their own good. Which is exactly why I want to remind you that the very best in the world are relentless at mastering the fundamentals. Kobe Bryant spent hours working on dribbling drills every day.

Dave Chappelle and Jerry Seinfeld practice comedy sets in small comedy clubs to this day.

And I still read books and get advice from people whose businesses are a fraction of the size of my own.

Here's why: First, you want to stay sharp. Second, you can always learn something from everyone, no matter what they do. And third, the bigger your business gets, the *more* impactful a single insight can be.

That last point is really important.

Let me show you with an example. When my business was generating $100,000/year, if I learned something that boosted my revenues 2%, that would equal $2,000.

(Interesting side note: If you consider the level that your business will probably be around in 5 years, that's missing out on $10,000 if you stay at your current level.)

Now, take that same insight and apply it to my business when it was generating $1,000,000/year, that same 2% was worth $20,000 in one year. And $100,000 over 5 years.

The bigger your business gets, the more the fundamentals matter.

That's why I want you to pay close attention to these lessons. Let's do it.

1. THE 3 SURPRISING RULES OF MONEY: BREAK THEM AT YOUR OWN RISK

Not long ago, we started to explore the fitness space to help men and women lose weight.

Some of our students had tried everything: Crossfit, Weight Watchers, Precision Nutrition, you name it...and said this was the ONLY time they managed to KEEP the weight off.

Interestingly, a lot of these students are massively successful in other parts of their life. But even though they invested time, money, and energy into their fitness, they couldn't "crack" it. One person told us, "This is it. If this doesn't work, I just have to accept this is my body and there's nothing I can do to change it."

We asked them, "What's your biggest fear about weight loss?" and one student admitted:

> *"I'm terrified that if I lose weight, I'll have saggy skin and actually look worse."*

In over 10 years, I've seen nearly everything...and I had to pick my jaw off the floor after reading this. It was so raw and real...

yet how many weight loss programs do you think talk about it? None.

They weren't just afraid of failing. They were actually afraid of succeeding.

In other words:

How can you achieve your goal if you're terrified of what you'll look like when you're successful?

What might you do to sabotage your success? Maybe you won't push yourself at the gym ("8 reps is fine, I don't want to injure myself.") Or you'll fudge the truth in your food journal ("It's the weekend, those cookies don't count.")

If you don't have your psychology right, it's 100x harder to succeed. It's true about fitness. And it's also true about money.

Understanding how money works—what I call the Surprising Rules of Money—is absolutely imperative...and something few people will ever tell you.

You can go online for yourself and read every blog post on making more money. You can read every business book in your library. They'll give you tactic after tactic after tactic.

Tactics alone will not help.

If we don't get our head straight about money, the best tactics in the world can't help you. That's why before you read anything else, I'm introducing you to the Surprising Rules of Money.

These rules took me years and years to master. You see, I was petrified of selling my first online product (I'll show you exactly HOW I got over this fear in Chapter 6: "What should I charge?": How to sell without feeling sleazy). It was a $4.95 e-book—and I was terrified people would call me a sellout. It took me years to be able to say, "You know what? My stuff is really good, and I'm going to charge for that and if you are not ready to pay, or you can't afford it, that's OK."

It took me years to master that. I see many other entrepreneurs who start, but as soon as it comes to making money, they get really scared. I totally understand.

Money is an emotional topic. It makes us feel guilty. It makes us feel alone. Who else can we talk to about it?

We start to say things to ourselves like: "I love doing this, why should I charge for it? I don't want people to think I'm greedy."

Or, "I enjoy this. Why should I even charge for it at all?"

These invisible scripts we have in our head act like an anchor tied around our neck, stopping us from making it to the next level because we're always terrified of what will people think

So here are the 3 Surprising Rules of Money. Don't worry if they don't fully sink in right now—it took me years to really "get it." But when you understand and internalize these, you'll see it's the difference between a business struggling to earn its first dollar...and a business that allows you to escape the 9-5 and live the life you want.

Rule #1: People Pay Me for the Value I Create

The world is not a zero-sum game.

You would not believe how many emails I get from people that say, "Oh, Ramit. So this is it? After getting 15 free emails from you, now I realize it was all leading up to a course that you're SELLING?"

Here's the most fascinating thing behind what they're really saying. Beneath the words is the belief: "If you make a dollar, I lose a dollar."

That's a scarcity mindset. People with a scarcity mindset believe there's a limited pie, and if you take one piece, that's one piece less for everyone else.

The truth is the pie can infinitely expand.

There are people out there who, if you can connect with them emotionally, if you can show them you've helped other people like them, if you can promise them the results they want, AND deliver, they'll pay you $1, $5, $500, $5,000...and they will be happy to do it.

The world is not a zero-sum game. Think about a time where you paid for something and you loved it.

What was it?

- A new cell phone?
- A trip where you stayed in a really nice hotel?
- An amazing meal with your boyfriend, girlfriend, husband, wife?

Did you sit there and think, "Ugh. I just paid $200. I'm never getting that $200 back." Or, did you say, "Wow. That was an amazing experience I'll never forget"?

Think of the things that you might be able to help other people with. Maybe you're a health coach. Maybe you can help people organize their homes or their lives. Maybe you can help them dress better, or you can help them grow their business.

Imagine every morning, your potential customers wake up and they think about that problem, virtually every hour of their day.

If you could solve that problem for them, once and for all, how much would they pay? $100? $1000? $10,000?

When you can connect and really solve their problems, the price is a mere triviality.

If I'm doing something really low-value, like spell-checking someone's essay, which Microsoft Word can do better than I can, then I probably shouldn't get paid much.

But what if I'm adding massive value to someone's life?

What if I change the way they look and help them feel better about themselves? What if I help them grow their business?

Then of course they're going to pay me for the value I create. They'll be thrilled to do it.

Don't worry about the HOW just yet. You'll learn more about that in the next chapter, How to uncover profitable ideas that virtually guarantee your business will work. For now, just remember that if you create value for others, they'll happily pay for it.

Rule #2: The More Money I Make, the More Value I Can Create

There's this idea that if you charge a lot and your business generates a healthy income, then you're just going to sit around, hoard your money, and swim through it like Scrooge McDuck.

That is not what successful entrepreneurs and business people do.

I've been accused of this myself: "Oh, Ramit just runs his business so he can make a lot of money."

Remember, making money is a byproduct of adding massive value to the world (Rule #1). But, how do you think I wrote a New York Times Bestseller based off a blog, built high quality courses, and created a world-class event?

By taking the money I make and reinvesting it back into making my business even better.

For example, each time we create a new course, I fly across the country to shoot the videos. I hire a professional film crew, book time at a professional studio, and rent professional cameras.

I also hire the world's best course creators, copywriters, designers, and technologists. Why? It's NOT just so I can sit around and hoard my money.

It's so that when you join one of my courses, you know you are getting the single best work ever produced on that topic.

If you join any program from *I Will Teach You to be Rich*, you know that it's been researched and been tested with typically 100,000 plus data points.

In other words, I take the money I make, and I reinvest it back into creating something even better.

Now, you can do the same thing. Let me give you a simple example:

When you start off, no matter what business you create, you may start with a very simple website.

As you earn more money, as you are more successful in helping your students, your clients, your customers, you can upgrade to a better website. You can hire customer support people to reach out proactively to your customers and ask "How's it going?" and "Were you able to find everything you wanted?"

You can hire people to help develop your ideas. You can hire a speaking coach. Maybe you want to hire a camera crew to follow you for a "day in the life of." Maybe you want to hire a designer to create an interior decoration plan so your videos look amazing. There are so many ways you can add value!

Remember:

The more money you make, the more value you can create.

This is SO important. For a lot of us, when we first start making money, we start off making $100, maybe $1000. That all soon starts to add up.

We start wondering: "Should I really be getting paid for doing something I love? Why don't I just share this with the world for free?"

The truth is, getting paid and sharing with the world for free aren't mutually exclusive. You can do both!

You can share what you do for free, but if you want people to truly take action, then you can offer a higher level offer. That's what I do: 98% of my stuff is free, and for those 2% who are ready, they go to the next level.

That 2% funds the entire rest of my business!

Rule #3: Money Is a Marker That I'm Doing the Right Thing

All of us know entrepreneurs who will literally use any number as a proxy for success...

They'll talk about how many readers they have. How many people like their Facebook page. Or how many Instagram followers they have.

They'll choose any sort of number they can...as long as they can avoid talking about HOW MUCH MONEY THEY MAKE.

Most entrepreneurs won't talk about revenue, because it's scary and it's intimidating. Which is precisely why we're talking about this now, in the beginning of the book. It's critical you nip this in the bud, before it becomes a "thing."

The best entrepreneurs know we have an OBLIGATION to ask for the sale, because that's the best way to help our customers. The best entrepreneurs know we have to avoid reporting the "fake" numbers and focus on the number that matters—sales.

For example, at a previous company I worked at, we did a deal with a very large internet company. They sent us a TON of traffic. I mean, they turned the traffic geyser on. We basically got thousands and thousands of new people every single day, like clockwork.

It was a gargantuan amount of people...

Can you guess how many of those people bought?

That's right. Not a single one.

Those huge spikes in traffic? They were fake numbers. We had tons of traffic and no sales.

I'd rather focus on the few real numbers that matter, like sales, revenue, profit, etc., than all these other proxies for success. Why? Why is money a marker that I'm doing the right thing?

Because it's not hard to get your customers to take the first step. You can get people into your store. You can get people onto your web site, or to read your blog. You can even get them to sign up for your email list.

But it takes a lot of trust for someone to actually pull out their wallet and pay you money, because they believe you can help them solve their problems.

Do that, and it means you've created something good enough that people say, "Yes, I need this!" When they pull out that credit card, you know they really mean it. They're not just saying they need it because they're worried about hurting your feelings.

So remember, it's normal to feel a little "weird" when you start making money. You're going to see that making sales is the ultimate benchmark for success. Not because you want to swim in a pool of dollar bills like Richie Rich.

Nope. It's because you know money is the marker you're doing the right thing.

Break These Rules at Your Own Risk

These Surprising Rules of Money took me years to internalize, but they're absolutely critical. I suspect that over time, after you've been out there in "the trenches," you'll revisit this chapter with a newfound appreciation for the rules.

For now, I strongly recommend bookmarking this page. If you're ever wondering WHY you should be starting your business, or why you should charge money doing something you love, this page will remind you.

Rule #1: People pay me for the value I create. In other words, if I create value, people will be more than happy to pay me for it.

Rule #2. The more I make, the more value I can create. I can invest back into the business, by building systems, creating technology, and hiring new people.

Rule #3. Money is a marker that I'm doing the right thing. We're going to avoid fake proxies of success, like how many

YOUR MOVE

people like my Facebook page. Instead, we'll focus on the ultimate sign that you've created something the world wants: Sales.

13

2. FINDING A PROFITABLE IDEA: THE SIMPLE PROCESS WE'VE USED WITH 20 PRODUCTS

I remember going to one of my first college parties as a freshman. It's a Friday night, and we're all hanging out in someone's dorm room.

People are drinking, some more heavily than others, including the guy who's dorm room we're in. He's pounding his seventh shot, going crazy, and I remember thinking, "Wow this dude's pretty wild."

Then I glanced over at his desk, and I see he left a textbook open: He's taking this neuroanatomy course, which was extremely advanced for a freshman.

"Huh, that's interesting," I thought.

Then I spotted a violin case in the corner. Later, I found out he's also a champion violinist! I was like, how is this even possible?

What I learned that night is that everyone has what I like to call an "X-Men ability": Something we're amazing at that we don't quite realize is special. Obviously, not everyone is a neuroscientist or world-class violinist—me included.

But the point is, we're all good at something…

And with some careful sleuthing into our X-Men abilities, we can take those skills and turn them into a business.

What Do You Already Pay to Learn?

Take 1 minute and read the below questions. Don't worry about writing anything down, just think about possible answers from your life.

Here we go:

1. **What are some things I already pay to learn?**
2. **What would I pay to learn if I could afford it, if money was no issue?**
3. **What's a problem I have that I'd pay almost anything to solve?**

What's the point of going through this exercise?

For many of us, we can't even conceive of the idea that someone would pay us for services. Most of our lives, our whole mental model of the world and how to make money has been pretty one-dimensional: Get a job, work 9-5, and collect a paycheck every 2 weeks.

There's nothing wrong with this model. For most people, it works fine. But as entrepreneurs and business owners, we're looking to break that model. Instead, our new model says, "You know what? I'm pretty good at something. I'm good enough that if I can find the right people, they will pay me."

At first blush, that seems like a very different way of looking at the world.

But in reality, we already do this.

Think of some of the things we already pay to learn. We pay for:

- College degrees
- Music instruction
- Wine tasting
- Personal training
- Yoga classes
- Personal development courses
- Certifications
- Learning Spanish
- Scuba diving

There are already things we pay for, and we happily pay! It's more efficient to pay money in exchange for someone's knowledge or expertise or skills. And if you're willing to pay for someone else's expertise, there are people out there who will pay for yours.

What if I'm Not an Expert at Anything?

The truth is, with 20+ years of life experience, you're guaranteed to be good at a lot of things. Sometimes they're just not immediately obvious: I call these our "invisible expertise." I'll show you how to uncover that expertise and turn it into a business, but first let me give you a simple example:

One of my students, Jarrett, is an interview coach who helps software engineers create a career they love. But do you think he has an "interview" degree or certification?

No! Jarrett is just a normal guy who's done a ton of interviews, he studied what works, and now he's sharing it with people like him.

"I am a software engineer, and my audience is other software engineers," Jarrett says. "So I know the language the people out there are working with."

When Jarrett first started, he thought he knew what his prospective clients wanted: An awesome career at Facebook or Google, that they would be proud to talk about with their friends and family.

But then Jarrett dug deeper. He started asking more and more questions, and he found out what software engineers secretly and desperately wanted—even if they were embarrassed to admit it.

Things like:

- "I've got a large amount of student loan debt. I want to make enough money to pay off my PhD."
- "I don't enjoy working on back-end systems anymore."
- "I want to start moving to mobile application development."

Jarrett could have let his "lack of credentials" stop him. Instead, he zeroed in on the exact words his market was using, and was quickly earning $700 per client with his interview business.

I brought Jarrett into the studio to get his full story. If you want to listen to our full 30-minute interview, go to growthlab. com/your-move.

Here are other examples where someone took their invisible expertise and turned it into a business:

- **How to Program With Java.** Tutorials on how to learn Java programming.
- **Bird Tricks.** How to train your parrot.
- **Learning Herbs.** Herbal medicine made simple.
- **The Ultimate Disney World Savings Guide.** Take a vacation to Disneyworld for half the price.
- **Hear and Play.** Play the piano without years of lessons and sheet music.
- **Fuzzy Yellow Balls.** Online tennis lessons.
- **Bony To Beastly.** Gain 20 pounds of muscle as a skinny guy.

As you can see, everyday people are turning their expertise into a successful business. However, your expertise is only one part of the equation. Let me show you the second part—the part that guarantees you'll have customers who can't wait to buy what you're selling.

Go Where the Fish Are

Fun fact: Indian people are not like white people.

We don't go hunting. We don't go camping. We don't play Frisbee golf. We don't even watch the Super Bowl.

So, when I was a kid and one day my dad woke me up and said, "Do you want to go fishing today?" I knew it was going to be a hilarious day.

He takes us to a fish hatchery close to our house. We don't know what's going on, but coincidentally we're there on the same day they're releasing a million fish.

We go to one part of the lake. We sit there, put our poles out and we're catching nothing. It's been 30 minutes, 60 minutes, nothing. We're getting kind of bored. We're starting to complain to my dad.

And my dad looks at us with a gleam in his eye. He says, "Come with me."

He walks us over to the actual pipe where thousands of fish every minute are coming out.

He says, "Put the pole there."

We do it, and we catch about 20 fish in 30 seconds. Great! Done for the day.

We got the fish, we go home, dinner is served.

I learned a lot that day.

Number one, my dad is a horrible fisherman. Only later did I learn how unsportsmanlike that is. Sorry fellow fishermen at the hatchery.

Number two, fishing became a lot more fun when I went where the fish were.

The same is true for your business. Shortcuts are like rare gems when it comes to business, and this "shortcut" is a 10 karat diamond: Go where the fish are. In theory, it's that simple.

However, speaking from personal experience, it's hard to always follow. For example, I:

- Taught a personal finance class in college to 20-year-olds who couldn't care less about keeping a budget.

- Created a program called "Scrooge Strategies" that taught frugal people to save money—an audience that by definition doesn't like to spend money.
- Spent thousands of dollars in R&D creating a health insurance product that got such a lukewarm reception, I never released it publicly.

These ideas were great. I had the expertise to teach them, and the know-how to package them into great products. Too bad none of that matters because NOBODY WANTED THEM.

Whatever your idea is, it has to be something somebody wants. Otherwise, you'll invest money and time building a business that only attracts looky-loos: Those people who come into your store, browse for 20 minutes, and NEVER buy anything.

This may be the most important idea in business. If you only take one thing away from this book, it should be this: **Create something that people WANT to buy.**

There are many audiences you should not build a business around, simply because they will never buy. For example, any business that serves nonprofits is doomed. Nonprofits are not going to pay you. Neither will restaurants or students. Restaurant owners believe they're "too busy" for most services, and students are poor and want to spend their limited money on alcohol.

A huge part of your success in business comes from consciously choosing who you're attracting and who you're repelling.

Let me walk you the exact step-by-step through the process I (and thousands of my students) use to find profitable ideas people want.

Finding Your Profitable Ideas

We're going to go through these next steps quickly, so you get the 10,000-foot view of how the process works. If you want to skim through the steps on your first read, go right ahead. When you're ready to dig deeper into the details, and get more step-by-step help on finding your profitable ideas, go to growthlab.com/your-move.

Step 1: Start with business ideas that suck

Here's the most liberating part of coming up with business ideas: You have permission to suck.

There are no bad ideas in the beginning stages.

I already showed you some of my early business ideas. They were terrible...But I've also gone on to create more than 18 successful products.

The first step to finding a profitable business idea: You have permission to come up with ideas that suck. Got it?

Once you've internalized this idea, you're ready to move on to step two.

Step 2: Ask yourself these 4 questions

It's easy to sit and create a list of random business ideas. But without the right framework, you can't tell if these ideas will ever pan out. That's why we use this simple exercise to get the ball rolling.

The first part of this exercise is to ask yourself 4 questions.

Question #1: What do I already pay for?

I like to lead with this question because a lot of us can't even fathom the idea that someone would pay us for something.

But when you think about it, we already pay other people for tons of random stuff.

For example, maybe you pay someone to:

- Clean your apartment
- Change the oil in your car
- Make your dinner

When you start to make your list, you'll quickly see that you pay other people every day.

That's why I start with this question. It opens your mind to what's possible when it comes to business ideas.

So take a second—right now—and think of about 3-5 things that you already pay for. Write them down on a sheet of paper and move on to the next question.

Question #2: What skills do I have?

What are you great at? Write those things down.

Remember, there are no bad ideas here. Your list of skills can include anything you want.

- Are you good at cooking?
- Do you speak Spanish?
- Are you an Excel whiz?

As you make your list, you'll start to see what people might pay you for.

For example: If you're great at cooking, maybe someone would pay you to be a personal chef for them.

If you know Spanish, maybe you could tutor someone.

If you're amazing at Excel, I know plenty of people who would gladly pay you to create some charts for them right now.

I want you to push yourself to come up with a list of at least 10 skills you already have.

Write down anything that comes to mind. Don't filter any of your ideas (remember Step 1: Start with business ideas that suck).

Once you've got at least 10, you can move on to the next question.

Question #3: What do my friends say I'm great at?

This is important because it can be very revealing.

Maybe your friends are always saying, "Wow, you give amazing relationship advice. You're the only person I come to." Or, "Your apartment is so organized. I wish my place looked like this." Or, "OMG, you're always wearing the perfect outfit! I'm so jealous."

You could turn all three of those things into successful businesses. Sometimes it's easy to forget we have these skills because they come naturally. And if you find yourself thinking, "Ramit, I do not have any skills," go ask your friends. It might seem a little weird, but I bet they'll give you a list of at least 3 things you're amazing at.

Add these ideas to your list. Shoot for at least 3-5 ideas and feel free to ask coworkers and family if you want. You might get different insights that way.

Trust me, you have many skills that have never even occurred to you.

Question #4: What do I do on Saturday morning?

This last question comes from my good friend, Ben Casnocha.

He said, "When you're trying to find a business idea, think about what you do on a Saturday morning before everyone else is awake."

- What are you reading? Fashion magazines? Fitness books?
- What are you watching?
- What one thing could you do all day?

Another way to think of this is: If you were locked in a room with a friend, what could you talk about for 3 hours straight?

This is a great way to expose ideas and passions. The things you would have a blast sharing with the world.

By the end of these 4 questions, you'll have at least 20 ideas written down. If you don't have 20, go back and ask yourself each question again until you do.

Once you get to 20, you're bound to have a few that you can turn into a profitable business today. If this is you, feel free to skip the next step and move onto the next chapter.

Step 3: Use the Demand Matrix to guarantee your success

We always test our ideas for profitability. That way we can virtually guarantee they'll be successful. And for that, I want to show you a tool we use called the "Demand Matrix." Here's what it looks like:

The Demand Matrix is a very simple way to take your 20 ideas from Step 2 and figure out which of them are worth your time.

Before we get to that, I want to explain how this chart works.

In the upper right-hand corner of the chart, you've got the Golden Goose. Ideas that fall under this section make GREAT businesses. That's because these ideas have the potential to get a lot of customers and command a high price. Think of companies like P90X and Apple's iPhone—lots of customers, pretty high price.

Then, in the bottom right-hand corner, you'll see Mass Market. Under mass market, you can still get a lot of customers, but you'll only be able to charge a low price. Think of famous books you might read, like The 4-Hour Workweek. There are a lot of customers, but the price-point is pretty low.

Next, in the bottom left-hand corner, you've got a Labor of Love. These are business ideas that have few potential customers and can only charge a very low price. Any business idea that falls in this category is doomed to fail—before it even starts. This is your weekend hobby that nobody would pay for (like my dream of teaching people how to eat spicy foods).

Finally, in the upper left-hand corner, you've got High End. This is still a great business option because you can charge a high price, but you'll likely have relatively few customers. Think about companies like Rolls-Royce and Prada.

See how it works? It's a great way to test your ideas for (1) profitability and (2) demand.

It's not meant to be super scientific. It's just a back-of-the-nap-kin way to find out if an idea has a chance of being profitable. There are no right or wrong answers.

To test for demand, just ask yourself, "Do a lot of people care about this?" If the answer is yes, then ask yourself, "Are people willing to pay a lot to solve this problem?" to figure out price. You'll quickly see where your different ideas fall on the chart.

It's pretty simple, but I want to make sure you go through each step thoroughly. Getting this right up front can save you thousands of hours over the long run.

By just taking the 3 steps above, you've put yourself ahead of 99% of people who think of an idea and spend years of time and tons of money before finding out it will never be profitable.

3. THE SECRET TO CREATING 100, 1,000, OR 10,000 LOYAL CUSTOMERS

A while back, I was speaking at a conference where a lot of people had an email list they were using to build a business.

So I asked them, "How many of you belong to multiple email lists?" Everybody raised their hand. Next I asked, "How many of you get multiple emails a day from these lists?" Everybody raised their hand.

I said, "How many of you believe if you replied to one of those emails, you would actually get a real response from the owner? The person who is ostensibly writing those emails?"

Just like that, everybody's hand went down.

Interesting.

Now you know I had to go in for the kill.

"How many of you are on my list?" About half the audience raised their hand. "And how many of you have ever replied to one of my emails and gotten a real reply from me?"

A pretty big percentage, probably 25%, kept their hands raised.

With that example, I wanted to show them what it takes to build a business that stands out. Not just going through the motions of listening to people, but *actually* listening to them. Engaging. Responding. Having fun with it.

By the way, that response made me proud to know that we're walking the walk, not just talking the talk. Authenticity matters, and people notice.

Actually listening is the critical differentiator between a successful business with happy customers...and everyone else.

It's easy to sit, write an email and blast it out to everyone. On the other hand, it's hard to actually listen to people. And I promise, that difference can be worth millions and millions of dollars. I cannot emphasize enough that the simple act of actually listening to people—without judgment—can skyrocket your business.

Now, trust me, I know that's not always easy. I have A LOT of personal issues with this. I used to be very overbearing, and it's something I've worked on a lot.

People would say something like, "I don't know what to do with my money, it's just sitting in my savings account." And like some poorly scripted super hero, I'd spring into action: "Hey! You really need to put it into a Roth IRA! You're losing potentially millions of dollars! Here, look at this compound interest chart!"

Have you ever watched someone's eyes just glaze over on you as they tune out your every word? Feels good, doesn't it?

Fortunately, there's a better way to help.

The Magical, Million-Dollar Words
It starts with these 4 simple words: "Tell me about that."

"You don't know what to do with your money? Tell me about that. What is the money doing right now?"

They might say, "Oh it's just kind of sitting in my savings account."

Then you can start teasing things out. I might say, "Well, what have you thought about in terms of what you could do with that money?"

"Well, I don't know I'm just overwhelmed," they'll say. "I have a lot of other stuff going on, I should probably do it one of these days." When you hear those words, that's your cue to twist the knife. For example, I'd say, "It must feel pretty tough, to have the money sitting around in a savings account with no idea what to do. I imagine it nags at you, in the back of your mind."

Just like that, by showing EMPATHY, the flood is unleashed, and they'll tell you everything:

"Yeah! My parents went through bankruptcy! I'm scared to do anything with my money" or "We grew up really poor so I was raised to always worry about money" or "My spouse handled the finances, and now that we're divorced, I'm not sure what to do."

And you're ACTUALLY LISTENING.

You're not trying to sell anything. You're just listening to learn.

This is how we uncovered major insights worth millions of dollars. Let me give you a quick example: What's the difference between...

"I want to make more money."

and

"I want to earn money on the side?"

At first glance, not much. But when we tested it, there was a HUGE difference—one that transformed us from a 6-figure to a 7-figure business. And we discovered this by listening.

How do you do this? How do you train yourself to listen to people in a way that:

- Creates successful customers
- Brings those customers back to you again and again
- And helps grow your business?

Let's go over some ways you can start today.

Make Sure You're Talking to Your Target Market

First, you want to talk to people who are in your target market.

These people can be friends, they could be family, but you want to make sure that these are the customers you'll actually serve.

For example, when I started "*I Will Teach You to be Rich*," if I had talked to people who were my parent's age, they would have said something like: "I wish I had saved for retirement earlier."

Now imagine if I took that and put it in front of a 22-year-old? Would they be itching to read my "Ultimate Guide to

Catching Up on Retirement?" Of course not! They don't want to hear anything about retirement!

Instead, I focused on my market: 22, 25, 30-year-olds, and they said things like:

- "I don't know what to do with my money, it's just sitting there."
- "I just want to make sure my money is working for me."
- "I want to be able to buy a round of drinks for my friends."

These are the words I heard over and over again, and these are the things you want to listen for, everywhere you go. In real life, when you're talking to your family, friends, or colleagues, your ears should perk up whenever you hear the words "I want," "I wish," or "I don't know."

When you're online or browsing on your phone, you're looking for these kinds of words, too. It can be in blog comments, online forums, Reddit, or Facebook.

But it's critical that you first narrow it down to the people who could potentially be in your market.

Dig Into Their Hopes, Fears, and Dreams
You know who your target market is. Now you're ready to ask them questions.

I already gave you the 4 simplest words you can use to get people to talk: "Tell me about that." Here are some other simple but effective questions to dig into their problems:

- What's going on?
- How do you think about this?
- How does it make you feel?

From these questions, you're looking for anything unusual or highly evocative. In other words, you're looking for people to explain their hopes, fears and dreams to you. For example, you might hear someone say:

> *"I'm so frustrated in my career. I just feel stuck, I feel like every year I get passed over for a promotion and the guy that they just hired, he's five years younger than me. Can you imagine how it feels to go into work every day?"*

This is pure gold. If you're listening, you can take notes, and use his exact words for a variety of things: sales copy, blog posts, or marketing material. But your job is to dig deeper: Tell me more. Who is this guy? What's it feel like to be passed over again and again?

And if he trusts you—if you are truly asking these questions because you authentically believe you can help him solve his problems—he'll tell you everything. He'll open up to you.

(On the other hand, if you're coming from a sleazy, scammy place, he's going to think you're some weirdo. So always start from a place of helping others. Most people are smart, and they can immediately tell if you're genuinely trying to help.)

Here's another example: Let's say you're a stylist. You're asking people how they think about clothes, and let's say you're talking to a potential customer who is a woman. The first thing you ask is, "Hey, tell me what you think about fashion?"

She might say something like:

> *"Honestly, I see these models and I have all these Instagram people that I follow. I know what I like but I can't actually figure out how to make my style fit that. And so every day I wear the same clothes and I just feel boring."*

Again this is pure gold. This is the kind of stuff you want to know.

If instead she just said something like, "Oh, I don't know. I'm just trying to up my style," well, that wouldn't be very good. It's boring. There isn't much you can do with that.

You want to get to know their hopes, fears and dreams. You want to get at the very evocative things people are feeling inside. The best part is, THEY WANT TO TELL YOU. They want to get this off their chest, IF you're willing to listen.

This single skill alone is a major differentiator for us. It's how we know precisely what customers want, and how we can solve it for them. We listen, grab all those insights, and write down real, juicy quotes into a simple document.

And it's been worth millions of dollars.

How Will I know It's Working?

Once you truly understand what your customers really want, and starting applying these insights to your marketing and sales material, amazing things begin to happen.

Your writing (whether it's your website or sales copy or marketing materials) will resonate with your customers. People will start writing you with messages like these:

"I feel like Ramit is personally talking to me in his emails…like he can read my mind. A little creepy, but effective, obviously."—Megan F.

"I was hooked. Hooked on the psychology behind everything, Ramit was in my head and knew exactly what I was thinking…"—Anthony P.

"I've been on your email list since early 2011. I never paid you a dime…however, this is exactly what I have been looking for and what I need. You are totally in my head and your sales page struck multiple chords with me."—Jesse S.

Once you've picked your target market and know their exact hopes, fears, and dreams, every word you put in front of your customers is surgical. One of my star students, Chris C., found this out with his tiny list…of 16 people.

Chris is an engineer who wrote about different problems he solved in a blog. Occasionally, he'd email these findings out to his list. He didn't have anything to sell, in fact, he only linked back to his website in one spot—in the footer, below his signature.

"I just put a link to my site there, and I kind of forgot about it."

He started getting email replies back from people, who said they read his blog and thought it was amazing. Then they started offering him consulting work.

"It was totally insane. It happened 4 or 5 times where people would say, 'Hey, I clicked on the link in your footer. Like, I was totally geeking out on your blog. I have this problem with my business. Can you help me out?'"

Chris was offered a total of $35,000 in consulting fees... from a tiny email list of 16 people, because he knew the exact hopes, fears and dreams of his audience.

Here's another example from one of my students, Diana:

> *"The things that my audience say to me are so validating: 'I love your voice—straight to the point, sassy and so you! Sometimes it felt like you were right inside my head!'*

> *"[Listening] allowed me to get a backstage pass to their private life and now that I have so much insight, it only continues to grow.*

> *The private emails I receive are so insightful and vulnerable and I honestly don't even have to come up with new content ideas. My readers bring issues to my attention."*

Be Selective of Who You Serve
One final note about serving successful, happy customers: You choose who you serve.

There's a great sushi restaurant in San Francisco where it's almost impossible to get reservations. If you try to walk in after 7:30 p.m., sorry—you're out of luck. When I finally got inside, like a true weirdo, the first thing I did was start analyzing how much revenue they were leaving on the table.

I'm sure they could generate 25% more revenue by squeezing more tables in. But they just don't care. They run their business the way they want to, and they have a line out the door every day.

I started to admire how they lived and breathed their style of business. If you weren't there early enough, sorry. If you asked for substitutions, you should probably try another place down the street.

(Of course, they had to have the best sushi to set these rules, which made their restaurant even more interesting to me.)

That attitude inspires me—to be able to run my business the way I want, and to be able to choose the customers I want to work with. To sacrifice short-term revenue to create a business I am proud of.

Over time, we've learned to be very selective about who we allow to join us. Notice we use the word "allow"—not to be arrogant, but because we spend millions of dollars developing and testing our material, we consider it a privilege to allow someone to join. For us, that means no customers with credit card debt, and nobody who hasn't spent a few weeks on our email list. By being selective, we can narrowly target the wants and needs of our market with pinpoint accuracy, and create products they WANT to buy.

We call this our "students for life" philosophy, and as you can see, it's highly profitable:

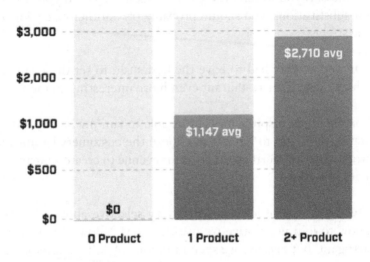

This chart tells us that once someone decides to become our customer, they're very valuable to us.

They're valuable to us because they tend to buy more than once and stick with us for a long time.

Marshall Goldsmith, one of the world's top executive coaches, put it to me this way: "Your biggest challenge [is] customer selection. You pick the right customer, you win. You pick the wrong customer, you lose. Focus on helping great people get better."

Ultimately, this is your business. It's up to you to run your business as you see fit, and serve the customers you want to serve. In our experience, business is the most fun (and most profitable) when you focus on helping great people get better.

4. FIELD REPORT: NOBODY'S A "NATURAL ENTREPRENEUR" BY DANNY MARGULIES

Danny Margulies is one of our star students who helps freelancers and aspiring freelancers make money on Upwork. You can read more about Danny's business and journey at growthlab.com/your-move.

For years, I was that guy.

The one who "never lived up to his potential." The one who bounced around from one dead-end job to the next, making little money:

- Restaurant manager—$20 an hour
- Appointment setter for a car dealership—$15 an hour
- Telephone interviewer—$15 an hour

I was the guy who spaced out at work, dreaming of my own business. Who never stopped annoying my friends with my ideas for the next big thing. But I thought I didn't have the brains, the genes, or the guts to succeed, so I did nothing. It felt safer.

Now that's all changed. It's 4 years later, and I'm making six figures from my business.

My website, FreelancetoWin.com, has generated over $230,000 in the past 12 months. It wasn't magic. It didn't happen overnight. I didn't meditate for hours hoping to "get in touch with myself."

No, I just studied successful business owners.

It turns out that real entrepreneurs don't think about starting a business like the rest of us do. And until you adopt their mindset, you will never be successful on your own.

Today I'm going to reveal the three most powerful lessons I learned in this process. These three simple mindset shifts will help you conquer your fear of starting a business and start thinking like a successful entrepreneur.

Mindset shift #1: There's no such thing as a "natural" entrepreneur

It's easy to get intimidated watching famous entrepreneurs. They seem like they were "born to succeed."

But it's an illusion. There is no "success gene."

For example, did you know that Mark Cuban's first job was bartending? Or that Sara Blakely failed her law school entrance exams and worked at Disney World before founding Spanx?

The reason famous entrepreneurs seem so natural is that, by the time you hear about them, they've had a lot of practice. Do you remember the first time you heard of Mark Zuckerberg? It was years after he started Facebook.

Want more proof that entrepreneurship is a learned behavior? Check out the chart below. It shows the first jobs of six of the world's most successful entrepreneurs:

Entrepreneur	First Job
Oprah Winfrey	worked at a grocery store
Michael Dell	sold newspaper subscriptions
Martha Stewart	babysitter
Michael Bloomberg	parking attendant
Jeff Bezos	McDonald's employee
Warren Buffett	newspaper delivery boy

It's not a superpower. It's a skill. Figuring that out is the first step every true entrepreneur needs to take. So start reading as much as you can about successful entrepreneurs' histories, paying particular attention to where they started, what they were doing before they "made it," and any failures they encountered along the way.

Ignore the media when they try to portray someone as an overnight success. To paraphrase Shark Tank's Robert Herjavec, "It takes 10-15 years of hard work to become an overnight success."

And whatever you do, don't compare yourself to billionaires. We all have to start somewhere! If others did it, YOU can do it, too. Steve Jobs once said, "Everything around you that you call life was made up by people that were no smarter than you."

Mindset shift #2: Mistakes are good

When we are children, we're taught early on to avoid mistakes. "Don't color outside the lines." "Why didn't you get an A on the test?" "Be careful not to spill that!"

But successful entrepreneurs love making mistakes, because it teaches them what to avoid in the future.

Take Elon Musk, for example. In January, his company, SpaceX, tried to land a rocket booster onto an ocean barge.

Unfortunately, one of the booster's landing legs malfunctioned, and the entire thing was destroyed.

You might think the event was an embarrassing failure. But check out how Elon reacted: "Well, at least the pieces were bigger this time. Won't be last RUD, but optimistic about upcoming ship landing."

RUD means "Rapid Unscheduled Descent"—AKA crash landing! Most people would have trouble staying this positive if their 10-speed got a flat tire, but Musk sees it as an opportunity to learn and make improvements.

New entrepreneurs need to embrace this mentality. Mistakes should be expected—nobody's perfect. Instead, use your mistakes to make positive change.

Since you probably won't be landing rockets any time soon, let me show you a quick example of a mistake I made a few weeks ago in my online business.

Last month, I sent a survey to more than 10,000 of my email subscribers to see if they'd be interested in buying a course about freelance blog writing.

But most of them didn't even understand what "freelance blog writing" means!

I received dozens of confused and frustrated responses, to my surveys. Responses that basically said, "I have no idea what you're talking about."

Five years ago, a response like this would have crushed me. But today, I don't let it get to me. I learned a valuable lesson. I never would have known that my readers don't know what "freelance blog writing" is had I not sent out the survey in the first place.

If you don't learn to embrace mistakes, you get stuck in analysis paralysis. You spend all your time thinking instead of acting. You can't grow a successful business that way any more than you can drive a car that's stuck in neutral. Some ways that have helped me overcome my fear of making mistakes:

Focus more on being decisive and less on trying to make the "right" decision. You'll never know until you try, and if you're wrong, you can always try again.

If a decision is reversible, try to maximize your gain. For example, last year I raised the price of my online course even though there was a chance I'd lose money if readers balked at the cost. The result: I quadrupled the previous month's revenue. And if I'd been wrong and people didn't buy, I could easily have changed the price back at any time.

Since the decision to raise the price was easily reversible—which meant my risk was practically nil—my only goal was seeing how big I could grow my business.

For irreversible decisions, try to protect yourself from losses. For example, imagine spending $5,000 on advertising, or giving away 50% of your equity to an investor. Unlike the previous example, you can't just change your mind if these decisions don't work out in your favor. So you need to be more conservative with these types of "bets." For this reason, guest blogging is my favorite way to build an online business—it's free, and anyone can do it.

And if you do make a mistake, go over it carefully to make sure you don't repeat it. The key is to figure out exactly what went wrong. Was your plan built on flawed assumptions? Did you execute poorly? Was it a failure of the last mile? Once you figure out the answers, you always win, regardless of the immediate outcome.

Mindset shift #3: Focus on giving, not getting

Typical wantrepreneur fears revolve around me, myself, and I.

"What type of business should I start?" "Will people buy from me?" "What will my friends think if I fail?"

This type of thinking sets you up for failure. Successful entrepreneurs don't focus on themselves—they focus on helping others. For example, you may have heard Ramit talk about how he gives away 98% of his material for free.

Back when I was stuck in a self-centered mentality, I came up with business ideas only I cared about, like a medical records faxing service no one needed and a new cat food no one wanted. Once I created a product designed to help other people make their lives better, 1,000+ people joined! Some of my blog posts have gotten hundred of comments and shares. And I've been able to get additional exposure for my business by guest posting on high-traffic websites in my industry like Business Insider, Copyblogger, and Upwork.

It doesn't have to be hard. Think about problems you've overcome in your career or personal life. Did you train your dog to walk without a leash? Are you ridiculously productive at work? Do you have 20 awesome hacks for overcoming anxiety?

Talk to people who are similar to you and see if they have the same problems. You can even start with friends and family to make it really easy.

Once you verify that others also have these problems, teach them how to solve them. You can do this with a blog post, a video course, or even through coaching sessions. By doing this, you're showing others that you want to help them improve their lives. That's how you build the trust that turns them into customers.

Make sure to follow up with the people you've helped, too. Once they've achieved measurable success, you know you have a proven system that you can confidently charge people to learn. And you also have a business that will succeed.

To become an entrepreneur, think like one.

Being a successful entrepreneur isn't magic. But it's not difficult, either. All it takes is a few simple changes to the way you think.

Once I began adopting these mindsets, I went from broke wantrepreneur to business owner in less than 3 years. A huge bonus of earning money this way is that I get to make a living by helping people improve their lives. Practically every day I wake up to messages from people I didn't even know beforehand, thanking me for helping them do work they enjoy, charge what they're worth, and enjoy more freedom.

PART 2: FOCUSING ON THE RIGHT THINGS

You can usually tell the difference in someone's expertise by the language they use. It's extremely telling and I find it fascinating.

For example, people who have just decided to lose weight are often fixated on random tactics: "Should I eat raspberry ketones? Do I need to eat right after my workout? What if I do high reps vs. low reps?"

But if you ask an experienced athlete, they'll say something like, "I eat right and train hard every day."

What's going on in these two statements?

The answer is that most of us—and most beginners—focus on the wrong things. We worry about minutiae that won't change a thing and mentally exhausts us.

Experienced pros have gone through this phase (it's natural, after all), and know what to pay attention to and what to ignore.

For example, should you eat right after your workout? Sure, it's probably a good idea. But it's 100x more important to get to your workout at least 3x/week.

I see this all the time in business. People have read some blog post about how they need a detailed analytics package, or they need to use Pinterest, or how they're going to die if they don't do recorded webinars.

You can safely ignore most of those things. In fact, I believe in doing less—and doing it better. Our business doesn't do half the things that many of our competitors do. Yet we're bigger than they are.

In this section, I want you to focus on internalizing the idea of focusing on the right things. Anyone can be "efficient"—meaning they can do a given task pretty well.

But very few can be "effective," meaning they select the right things to work on in the first place.

Focusing on the right things is a true superpower. Let's dive in.

5. BEING DIFFERENT: THE ART OF STANDING OUT FROM THE CROWD

Have you ever noticed how the minute you start trying something new, the entire damn world tells you what you should do?

If you've ever tried to change your diet, you know what happens: Your boss, your aunt, and your garbage man all start giving you their advice:

- "Do Paleo! It's the best way to lose weight."
- "Don't bother, our family is just big boned. It's genetics."
- "The only thing that worked for me is this green juice cleanse."

The exact same thing happened to me when I first started my business. Most people ignored the excellent content, or that I was telling people the exact word for word scripts they could use to get themselves out of debt.

Instead, they told me:

- No one would take such terrible design seriously
- To go buy people McDonald's meals so I could ask them personal finance questions
- That the name of my site (and book) sucked

I remember thinking two things: First, never go to the general public for business advice. Everyone thinks they're a business expert after watching Mark Cuban for 30 minutes on Shark Tank.

Second, I thought that if I ran and grew my business and was successful, all the critics would shut their mouths and bow to my feet. Man, I was so naive back then.

After more than 10 years of running my business, I discovered the more successful you are, the MORE critics you get...and the criticism just gets more inane:

- "Ramit, you really need to get on Facebook."
- "LOL $99? Maybe I'd buy it if were $0.25 and had a 30-year-guarantee."
- "So you're just one of those scammy e-book guys who writes those long sales pages?"

Here's an unexpected lesson I learned: The world wants you to be vanilla. They will always push you to look and act the same as everyone else.

If your business is going to stand out and succeed, it's up to you to push back.

"Will I Make it into Your Top 50?"

I once spoke on a panel in Napa Valley called "What I've Learned in the Last 10 Years." During the presentation, one of the other panelists said something that did NOT go over well. I found it fascinating.

This guy is a successful entrepreneur. He was talking about how, as he's gotten busier, he's had to change how he maintains his relationships. He's realized he'd rather nurture his existing relationships than take random coffee meetings or meet with random people.

OK, cool. That's a pretty honest statement. He has limited time and wants to spend it with people he knows.

No problem so far...

So he finally figured out what works for him: He created a "Top 50 Favorites" list of contacts on his phone. He prioritizes them when it comes to hanging out. When he has a free minute, he calls/texts the people on his Top 50 list.

Then he told us, at the end of the year, he re-evaluates who should be on the list and shuffles/deletes/adds to it. It can only be 50 people, so every year, he makes the tough decisions as to who's in his Top 50.

People DID NOT LIKE THIS. You could hear it in the audience—everyone went silent and there was almost a collective gasp. Later, during Q&A, most of the questions were half-jokes about, "Will I make it into your Top 50?" In a room that was otherwise warm and welcoming, this felt opportunistic and transactional.

Personally, I loved it.

He's a guy who is busy and has to make tough choices. Trust me when I tell you he's a very nice guy who wants to help people. But he also knows what it takes to grow his business. Here's the vanilla answer everyone hoped to hear: "You just do the best you can!" or "I try to help everyone!"

But when he was actually honest about what it takes to succeed at a higher level, people couldn't stomach it. They would have preferred if he was vanilla.

"I Just Watch What I Eat"

Here's another example, totally outside of the business world: One of my friends is a mother of 3. She told me how other women would ask her how she looked so amazing with her busy job and family of 5. She used to excitedly tell them about her detailed workouts and diet. Their response? "They got really mad," she told me. They would say things like, "I could never do that," and "Must be nice to have time."

You know what she tells them now? "I just watch what I eat and play with my kids a lot." And they smile and carry on.

She gave them the vanilla answer they wanted: "Just watch what you eat! Move your body!"

Her friends didn't want to hear about the discipline it took to wake up at 5:30 a.m., workout, prep food, and get the kids ready for school, THEN go to work. It made them feel bad. Easier to just give the vanilla answer than start a fight with our friends.

Should We All Just Discover Our Calling?

Last example: I recently read an interview of this big-name CEO. Someone asked him, "What advice would you give to someone who wants to do what you do?"

"My number 1 piece of advice to people is to discover their calling."

Now just step back and think about this advice. It sounds logical, right? It even feels good. We need to find our passion, find our calling, do what we love…

...but if we dig deeper, we'll notice all the things he *didn't* say:

- He never watches Netflix and doesn't even own a TV
- Every Sunday evening, he spends 3 hours in the office planning out his week
- He's *always* thinking about work. In the shower, while buying coffee, and yes, while eating with his family

Why didn't he say all of this stuff?

Because most people don't want to hear about the hours he puts into working every single week. That sounds hard! It's much easier to drop a vanilla sound bite that people can feel good about—even if it's not 100% true.

The world wants you to be vanilla...

Yet the greatest irony is that the moment you give in and start to conform is the same moment everyone abandons you.

Perhaps you charge less, because someone said they wouldn't pay you more than 20 bucks. Or you change your website design so it blends in with all the other businesses in your niche. Or you adopt the same, sanitized copy the corporate big boys use.

In a world full of websites and e-books and apps, the moment you look and sound like everyone else, you're dead.

Avoid The Commodity Economy

Salt is what's called a commodity. It's called a commodity because you don't care which brand of salt you get...they're all the same to you. You can substitute one brand of salt for another and nobody would be able to tell the difference. And as a result, the price of commodity salt is extremely low.

When we let ourselves and our businesses become vanilla, when we try to appeal to everyone, we instantly become a commodity.

I understand how tempting it is to run the same business as everyone else. If everyone else is getting business cards, creating logos, or targeting similar markets, they must be doing it for a reason, right?

It's scary to say "No." It's scary to pass when everyone else is doing it, and potentially close the door on lucrative opportunities. Most of our lives, we've been taught to stick with the herd and not to stand out. As Michael Ellsberg pointed out to me, "Our parents were concerned with keeping us safe." Which makes sense. They told us to not take too many risks, to fit in, and jump through the hoops. It's great advice if you're prioritizing safety.

Michael said, "It's not great advice if you want to be excellent, because by definition, excellence is sticking out from the herd. It's excelling ahead of everyone else."

But imagine you have a burning problem you need to solve. In fact, you'd pay any amount of money to make this problem go away. For example:

- You're a skinny guy looking to gain muscle (like I was), would you rather go to a trainer who specializes in "beginner bulk up" or a trainer who works with new moms, guys looking to lose weight, and senior citizens?

- You're looking to buy a rare collector's Corvette, are you going to go to the general used car lot or a specialty dealer?
- You want to learn woodworking, will you learn from a craftsman or a handyman?

Think about each of the options presented. Which do people seek out? Where do they spend more money? Of course, with the specialist. The person who stands out.

That's the way your business wins in a world of vanilla. By standing out.

Say It Another Way

Whatever your business, chances are you're facing tons of competitors. And standing out is the only way you can compete.

Look at my business: I was writing about personal finance.

By the time I arrived on the scene, effectively everything under the sun had been said about personal finance, right?

- "Spend less than you earn"
- "Save money"
- "Cut back on things like lattes"

But none of that resonated with me! It went in one ear and out the other, and I saw the same thing happening with my friends.

So I read all the best books on personal finance. I watched all the shows. Eventually, I realized there were plenty of different ways to package the information so that I stood out and helped the audience I wanted to help.

Early on, it was how I talked about certain things. I didn't just say, "Cut back on everything! Stop wasting money!" Instead, I said, "Spend on the things you love guiltlessly, while cutting costs ruthlessly in the areas that you don't." See how different that is?

I covered classic personal finance information, like low-cost investments, savings accounts, and Roth IRAs. But I also covered automating in a way that no one else had—because that's what my audience wanted. They wanted everything to "just work" so they could get on with their lives.

Focus on Your Customers, Not Your Competition

One student asked me how her yoga business could stand out. "There's so much common yoga knowledge out there. There are the basics of sun salutation, basic postures, some breathing, and some info on stretching."

This student lives in a big city like I do, and I get why she's worried. Everywhere you turn, a new yoga studio is popping up. How can she stand out in such a crowded market?

First, think deeply and differently: What are all the other issues when it comes to yoga that she could talk about? Of course, you have to cover the basic poses and stretching. That's the cost of admission. But what else?

How about...getting your boyfriend or girlfriend to join you in your practice? What about nutrition? What do the world's best yogis eat?

What about equipment? Are the very best in the world using something different than what a Manhattan executive uses in her class after work?

There are a million different ways to approach any topic. The key is: Instead of focusing on the competition, focus on your audience.

Who is your audience, and what do they want that they are not being served right now? I guarantee you, in the yoga audience, there are people who have never done yoga. Then there are people who tried it a couple times, and they kind of gave up. They say things like, "I should go back," but they haven't.

What you can do is take your special insight and your perspective on the world, and serve their needs.

That's how you build a business that stands out from all the rest.

Stand Out by Dropping Some Extra Fucks

My friend Tim Ferriss and I were talking about business, and he mentioned he was worried that if he sent an email without concrete takeaways, he'd have massive unsubscribes.

I reminded him: People signed up for your list for a reason. They would love to hear the stories of lessons you learned, failures you had, what happened this weekend, and interesting insights that came up.

The same is true for any business, brand, or writer. Not everything is transactional. Not everything is "how-to." A lot of times, people are happy to share stories and interesting ideas.

And for the people who unsubscribe from your list, or choose not to do business with you because you shared your ideas, here's how I think about it: It's my gift to you and it's your gift to me.

If we're not a good fit for each other, I wouldn't want to waste someone's time, and I don't want them to waste my time either. That's why I regularly encourage people to unsubscribe. I put the link right there. I say, "Look, if this is too much, if this is too involved for you, here. Maybe we're not right for each other. Unsubscribe."

And people do! Tons of people unsubscribe, because who says that? But the people who do stick around, they're highly committed and engaged and they ultimately buy from the business.

Tim laughed and told me he sometimes does something similar:

> "If I've had a long day and maybe too many glasses of wine, I'm like, 'You know what? I'm going to write a blog post and I'm going to put a couple of fucks in there, because I'm so tired of people chastising me for my language.'

> "So I'll write a post and drop a few extra few fucks, just so that if someone is easily offended by that stuff, they effectively opt out of visiting the blog because I don't want to deal with their mom-like scolding."

Stand Out By Becoming Obsessed

Author, journalist, and psychology expert Charles Duhigg says one of the best ways to stand out is by "indulging in your obsessive compulsive disorder."

"People who are successful are people who are not ashamed to say, I am super passionate and interested in X and I'm going to indulge that. Yes, I'm a weirdo. But I'm going to figure this out, and I'll figure out what I like about it, so that I can share it with you."

Think about the most successful people you know:

Elon Musk was obsessed with battery and solar power, which led to creating Tesla. Howard Schultz was obsessed with the barista/customer relationship he discovered in Italy, which led to Starbucks. Steve Jobs was obsessed with functional yet beautiful design, which led to Apple products like the iPod and iPhone.

They stood out to the world because they became obsessed.

I've found out that people who I went to school with—who are now successful entrepreneurs—indulge this obsessive compulsive disorder.

Stand Out by Setting the Bar Higher

I talk a lot about how I don't accept students with credit card debt, because it's important everyone knows this rule before trying to join a course.

But most people don't know about all the courses I run. At any given time, I'm launching and testing different ones for months—or even a year—before I mention them publicly. This way, when I do a public launch, I know my products are 100x better than anyone else's on the market.

Years ago, I was running a course called *Beyond 1K*, a follow-up to my *Earn1K* course on earning money on the side.

It was generating several thousand dollars a month—most of it pure profit—but after a year of testing, I wasn't satisfied with the results I was getting, or the results I was generating for my students.

So even though students continued to pay me a LOT of money, I shut it down. Here's the email I sent:

I wanted to let you know that I've decided to discontinue Beyond 1K—tonight will be the last Ass Kicking call—and I wanted to share my reasons for doing so.

My entire philosophy revolves around Big Wins—focusing on the most important and highest-performing actions you can take.

Not only do I apply this to my personal finances, I also apply it to my personal life (my Tripod of Stability) and my business.

To be blunt, Beyond 1K is not performing to the levels I want it to. I only want to create the best products, and focus on the highest and best use of time—for me AND for you.

I also want to take a minute to highlight the meta-lesson here. I've got a fully automatic system that is paying me lots of money each month with Beyond1K. It would be easy for me to coast and continue making several thousand dollars per month from Beyond 1K, but that's not what I want to do. That's not a Big Win for me or for you.

Sometimes you have to cut things out of your life that are performing well…just not as well as you WANT them to.

When I shared this news with a couple of friends (who don't know my business too well), they were shocked. "Why don't you just keep it running?" they asked.

They don't understand the idea of only focusing on things that are providing EXTREME value for my students and for my business. I can provide "good" value and be a mediocre performer. But I want to only provide EXTRAORDINARY value. I'd rather refund your money and focus on something that is going to take you 5 levels forward.

That's why Earn1K is so good (and costs so much).

And that's why I'm going to be working on several new products that are of such extraordinary quality, you've never seen something like it before.

As usual, you put your trust in me, and I want to honor that. I'll be refunding any unused money for Beyond1K. Any amount paid for Beyond1K after 11/21/2010 will be refunded in full. If you purchased the annual subscription of Beyond1K, you will receive a refund as well. You will get an email with the exact amount from the B1K team in the next 2 days.

Thanks, and I appreciate your help, support, and trust.

—Ramit

That email cost me over $75,000. And I'd do it again tomorrow, because I put the success of my students above profit. That's how we stand out in our world, where most people are just looking to make a quick buck.

(By the way, that's not lip service. I've shut down multiple products because I felt they underperformed and under delivered—even when they generated over $1,000,000. You can read more about it at growthlab.com/your-move.)

Don't be Different for the Sake of Being Different

I spent this entire chapter urging you to stand out, and showing you how different companies do it. Now, just a final word of warning:

Be different to be better. Don't be different for the sake of being different.

I once had a friend tell me he wanted to charge $62, an unusual price, for his product.

"Why?" I asked.

"I just want to try something new."

My friend was being an idiot.

There's no need to reinvent the wheel! Most things in business are remarkably similar. If you have a physical store, you need a property, signage, and goods to sell.

If you have an online business, you need a website, an email list, a sales page, and a product.

Get those basic things right, and you will grow. You don't need to reinvent the wheel on everything.

The most successful entrepreneurs—the top 1% of the top 1%—learn when to break the rules. It's like when you learn how to dress well and you start experimenting with patterns and textures because you want to. One day, someone's going to say, "Dude, that doesn't even match," and you'll say, "So?"

It's the same with your business. Know the best practices, execute them. Then, when you understand the rules and why they exist, you can start to break them. But don't be different for the sake of being different.

Do Business Your Way

I thought that as I ran my business, I'd learn about the super-secret tools that successful entrepreneurs used once they made their first $10,000, then $100,000, then $1,000,000 and beyond.

But actually, I learned two very different lessons:

My first lesson was that business isn't just about creating money. Of course, you need to get paying customers. And when you launch, you should be fiercely focused on building an audience of people who love what you're doing (and are delighted to pay). Ultimately though, every successful entrepreneur I know looks for more meaning than another $100 of revenue.

My second lesson was that you can create a business your way. There will always be people who criticize you for charging too much. Let them complain. They're not buyers.

There will be people who tell you that you "need to" set up a Facebook page, or Twitter account, or Instagram. I didn't have those for years. And even if you took all my social media accounts away today, it would make zero difference to my business.

We're fortunate to continue to grow, to continue to hire, and create new products. All the tools we have helped. The tactics mattered. But ironically, this didn't come from chasing revenue. Instead, it came from running the business our way. It came from standing out when everyone else was doing the same things, and never swaying from our core beliefs.

6. "WHAT SHOULD I CHARGE?": HOW TO SELL WITHOUT FEELING SLEAZY

Many beginning entrepreneurs and business owners start out feeling the same way about one thing: They're terrified at the idea of selling something.

They think:

- "I don't want to annoy people."
- "Will people think I'm only after money?"
- "Why would anyone want to buy from me?"

I've noticed that these beginning business owners and entrepreneurs then price their products or services out of fear. They say things like, "I just want to start off at a smaller price. That way people can get their feet wet. I don't want to be too salesy."

And I can put myself into that same bucket. I had a ton of fears when I started creating my first product. To be completely honest, I was petrified.

When I put this first product together, I felt like I went above and beyond for the time. This was in 2004, before you had sites like 99Designs or Fiverr where it was easy to get an e-book put together.

I had it beautifully illustrated. I put together a nice design. I sold it for $4.95, thinking I was doing the market a favor by giving it away so affordably. I called the product, "Ramit's 2007 Guide to Kicking Ass."

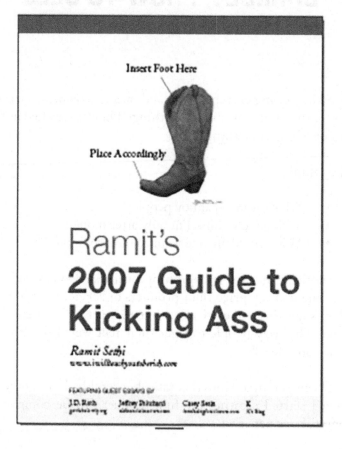

And if you read the copy, you could tell I was petrified of sell-ing it. IN THE SALES PAGE, I wrote:

"Why don't I just give this away for free? Couldn't you just find a lot of this stuff on Google?"

It was so cowardly, I cringe thinking about it now. But that's just how terrified I was of looking like a sleazy salesman.

Years later, I sell $2,000, $5,000, even $12,000 products...and I do it in a completely different way. I might say, "Look, this probably isn't right for you, let me tell you why. But for those of you who are ready to take the next step, the chosen few, this might be the right consideration."

It's a totally different mindset. The fears I had back then were things like: Am I charging too much? What if people think I'm a scam or a fraud? What if nobody buys, or worse, they buy, and then they think it's BS and then they refund?

These fears were paralyzing for me. They're paralyzing for A LOT of entrepreneurs.

For example, when my student, Danny M., first got into sales, he was working at a car dealership. No surprise, it left a bad taste in his mouth:

"Selling meant squeezing as much money as possible out of each person who walked through the door."

So the first time he sent a sales email, he expected the worst: "Everyone will think I'm trying to make money off them, and they won't believe a single word I say."

However, this pitch to his email list was different than his car selling pitches. This was HIS product. He believed in it. So his message was genuine, not filled with hype and scarcity tactics.

Hours later when orders starting trickling in, Danny realized his readers saw value in what he was offering. Even better: "Almost no one asked for a refund. And many of them sent me 'thank you' emails. It was a major paradigm shift for me."

When you conquer these fears, it's like this mountain of pressure suddenly moves off your chest. You can talk to your family, friends—and most importantly, your customers—about your business with confidence. You'll know that for most people, your product or service won't be right for them.

But for the right customer, it's like music to their ears, and they'll be begging you to take their money.

In Danny's case, he carried that fear of selling for years. I was the same way. It took me years to mentally get past these fears and feel comfortable selling such high value information products. I want to show you the shortcuts on conquering those fears, by teaching you some of the themes that came up over and over again for me.

These really changed the way I thought about selling, and it actually taught me that I'm doing the market a favor by creating high value products, and charging accordingly.

People Value What They Pay For

When my business first started doing well, my friends would say to me, "Ramit, can you give me a course for free?" And I always said yes.

I was raised in a culture where you help everyone you can, for free, and you don't expect anything in return. If you're a college guidance counselor, that means you're looking at all your nieces' and nephews' college admission essays. If you're a doctor, it means you can count on your auntie dropping off her X-rays for your second opinion. And if you sell information products, it means you give them access, no questions asked.

I never minded giving them access. I wasn't concerned about "capturing all the revenue." Plus it didn't really cost me anything to add another email address to my user list, so why not.

But...I would always track to see whether they logged on? Can you guess if they did or not?

The answer is: Of course not. People value what they pay for.

This sounds so obvious, but I didn't internalize it until this happened over and over again. I gave them a $2,000 course for free, they didn't even log in ONCE. After awhile, I started to feel a little resentful. This is my business. This is what I do and they're not even taking me seriously.

I tried to find creative ways to get them to put some skin in the game. It was important to me they didn't think I was greedy, that it was all about the money. But I also wanted them to take it seriously! I tried to get them to donate 50% of the sales price to charity, and I'd give them the course.

As you can imagine, that was a disaster.

Finally, I gave up, and whenever someone asked for a free program, I said, "Look, I want to give you this material. I know it can help you. It's not about the money, but in my experience, if people don't pay, they just don't value it."

I said, "This is my livelihood. This is what I do for a living and I'm really good at it. So, if you're interested, I'll be happy to open up a slot in this course. It's closed right now, but I'll open one up for you. But I would have to ask you to pay the full price, just like anyone else."

What do you think happened? Most of those people who wanted it for free went away. But the people who said, "Okay, I'll do it," they looked at every single lesson in the course. And that changed everything.

Remember: People value what they pay for.

> *"Nearing the final portion of the call, the prospect said: 'Okay, I've gotten so much already out of today and I know I want to work with you.' I then proceeded to discuss my recommendation and what working together would look like—a 3-month contract. Then the price: $2,600. EXCEPT, not only did they not bat an eye, they locked in to $2,600 PER MONTH for 3 months, totaling $7,800. What?!! I couldn't believe they saw that value in me. Yet they did."*—Jessica E.

I can tell you from our own data, that of all the people who get our free emails, the people who actually bought a product are 5 times more likely to open it than those who've never bought.

Think about that: On many of my paid lists, I have an open rate of over 100%.

That means they're opening up every email, more than once, whereas the typical email open rate on a typical list might be something like 15-18%. It's a stark difference.

Understand that people value what they pay for. You're not doing them a disservice by charging them, you're actually doing a profound service for the people who want to take action.

I'm Not Building for Everyone, Just the Right People

For years, I just assumed the more popular my site became, the fewer critics I would have. I naively thought people would see the thousands of students whose lives we changed, and they'd think, "Oh, I guess I was wrong about this Ramit guy. Plus, he's got magnificent eyebrows."

In reality, the more the business has grown, the MORE critics there are coming out of the woodwork. I find this fascinating. If you Google "Ramit Sethi," you're going to find a few people who say, "Oh, this is crazy. Ramit only talks about earning more because he wants to earn more for his stuff."

Or they'll say, "He started off teaching about frugality, but he quickly realized he could make more money from these high priced courses. You can tell it's a total scam."

At first that made me really uncomfortable because that's not why I create high-value material. I create high-value material because people value what they pay for. But over time, I realized something. All these people are out here criticizing on the internet, and my students internally, in our private groups and communities, are getting insane results. It was a stark difference.

These critics on the outside, people who basically troll, they love writing comments criticizing others. Meanwhile the people who have taken action are busy getting five, ten, twenty-five thousand dollar raises, launching online businesses, and becoming freelancers.

One day, I thought to myself, "Who do I want to pay attention to?" Is it the critic, or is it the people who are actually getting results? That one thought really put things in perspective for me.

Felicia S. felt the same way. She already had a successful business as a charisma coach, but she was scared to death of raising her rates. "I thought I was asking for too much. I thought people would balk."

And the moment she made her announcement, Felicia discovered she was right. "All of the things I was scared of DID happen. People unsubscribed and they balked at my rates."

"But that didn't affect my business. Many still bought from me and loved my products and coaching."

That's the thing about fears. Most of them are stories we tell ourselves. And no matter what you do, there are always going to be critics. Maybe they don't like how much you're charging. Maybe they can't afford it. Maybe they don't like the color of your hair. It doesn't really matter.

You can only focus on the people who are taking action. You can only try to change the world one person at a time with your business.

Learning Before Earning

The information product space is an interesting one. It's probably the only place where people will come in and say, "How do I earn money? I need to quickly earn $5000 a month in passive revenue."

Could you imagine a lawyer saying something like that? Or your accountant? Of course not, it's ridiculous. But with information products it happens everyday. So you see these people jump into the market and create these shoddy products. Maybe they make a hundred, or even a thousand dollars, but in a very short period of time, they disappear completely.

That is not what I pursue in my business, and I drill this into my students each chance I get: You have to learn before you earn. If you're reading this, I expect you feel the same.

It's critical you learn before you earn. If you learn the principles of business, if you build an amazing product, or a store that people flock to, if you target the right audience and find the people who will pay, then package everything in a way that makes people want to buy...

Then you keep those insights forever.

You can use those insights to create a $5 product, a $50 product, and a $5000 product. You can use those insights to sell T-shirts, open a dental practice, or flip action figurines on eBay. When you learn before you earn, all avenues of business are open to you, and you keep that for the rest of your life.

Meanwhile, all the other people who rush into the market, who try to quickly create a product that has no real value, they might make a little bit of money, but they'll be out of the market before you know it.

Don't be Apologetic

One of our writers at GrowthLab.com, Joe Choi, shared this example of how he looked at selling. It was so good, I included it here. Joe, take it away:

Imagine you had to convince someone to try your favorite restaurant or listen to a great new artist you just discovered on Spotify. Would you be shy about it? What would you say?

"Errr...this restaurant is okay. You can probably make the food on your own, but try it anyway! You might like it...I don't know..."

"I like this music. You might not like it, but listen anyway. Maybe if you have time?"

No way. You would unapologetically explain why your friend NEEDS to eat there. You'd talk about the atmosphere, service, and how amazing the food is. You also wouldn't hold anything back about the new artist. You'd explain why the sound is so distinct. Or compare this artist to another one that your friend loves.

It sounds silly when you put it this way. So why would you apologize to people before you pitch a product that can solve their problems?

Take Cal Newport and Scott Young. Normally we protect the innocent and don't call people out for mistakes they made. But since they're friends of GrowthLab.com, and we've pointed this out to them already, their example is a great one to learn from.

They released a course called Top Performer, which is all about using deliberate practice to master rare and valuable skills to get ahead in your career.

Imagine being one of the best at what you do for a living —a top performer. What would your life be like?

Top Performer is a course taught by Cal Newport, author of So Good They Can't Ignore You, and Scott Young. The course teaches you how to deeply understand your career and then develop the kind of career capital you need to become a top performer.

One of my friends (and a student in their pilot program) said it was amazing and one of the best courses they've ever taken.

But Cal and Scott didn't sell it that way.

Here's an apologetic call to action they posted:

> "I'll post another short note around 24 hours before the end of the sign up period. But that's the last I'll talk about this for a while. I know online courses is not everyone's cup of tea. If this includes you, please ignore this—we'll be back to our regularly scheduled programming shortly."

While this message seems like a harmless public service announcement, it only brings out the complainers and freebie seekers. Here's just one of the comments Cal and Scott got back:

> *"Cal—Thanks. I must say this has the look and feel of some sort of effort to build your email list. You've been successful in part because you're not too salesy. This feels like you want to create a Tim Ferriss-type email list for marketing purposes."*

Look, the fact is, some people will NEVER buy from you. Apologetic messages only seem to please the non-buyers. Their complaints poison the well for your real customers. Your real customers will be relieved that you have something worthwhile for them.

Luckily Scott found redemption when he posted this message on his blog:

Top Performer, Cal Newport's and my course on developing the skills to build the career you love, is now open.

Over four years ago, Cal and I were discussing two observations about career development. The first, is that having an excellent career depends on becoming really good at things the world values. That's true for all professions, whether you're a programmer, artist, manager or entrepreneur. The second, is that getting really good can often be a frustratingly difficult process. People stay stuck at the same level of skill for years, or they get caught up maximizing abilities that don't matter that much.

This simple idea led to years of work, multiple pilot courses and well over a thousand individual students. The result is Top Performer, a course we're both proud to offer that can guide you through the obstacles to becoming the best at what you do.

If that idea interests you, click here to find out more about the course. We'll be holding registration open until Friday, May 20th at 11:59pm PT. After that, we'll be closing registration to start the first week of the course with the new students on May 22nd.

Notice how it's not apologetic? And how it's not a high-pressure sale? He's just saying, "Hey, I put a lot of work into this thing. For the right people, I think it'll be valuable. Check it out." That's all selling is.

Pricing is Strategic

Many of us think that we just arbitrarily choose a price, slap it on the product, and it sells. In reality, it's much more sophisticated than that. Let me show you:

Take a fast food restaurant like McDonald's. McDonald's doesn't just choose $1 to $2 for their products randomly. They are one of the most sophisticated pricing technicians on the planet.

Because once they decided to go in at the low-cost entry option, everything around their business became focused on supporting exactly that.

What does that mean, "support the low-cost entry option"? It means, foolproof machines that untrained labor can use. It means documentation for everything, for when to flip the burgers and how much of a soft drink to pour. When you first start working at McDonalds as a 16-year-old high school student, all this documentation needs to be written in very clear language.

McDonald's also pays low wages. Why? They can't afford to pay more because of the margins they make on their products. They have built their whole business around a low-cost model, and it works very well for them.

Let's take another brand on the opposite end of the spectrum: Louis Vuitton. Louis Vuitton sells high-end handbags and fashion at high prices. We're talking about thousands of dollars for a handbag. They didn't just randomly choose that—pricing is part of their strategy.

It means that they have better material than a handbag you might find at TJ Maxx or Ross. It means that their material is handmade. So it's not just better material, but the products are actually handmade. At Louis Vuitton, they have better trained staff. They have different branding. You'll almost never see discounts or promotions, ever.

Pricing isn't just the sticker price. It informs your entire business.

Most people price out of fear. They just choose a price which is usually way lower than they should charge, and then they hope that no one notices they're actually charging money for this product. Your pricing signifies who you are and what kind of customer you want.

> "I talked to the first friend and floated the idea by them. I said I'm looking to coach people 1-on-1 through every step of [a specific niche]. From finding an idea to writing it and driving traffic to it. Everything.
>
> They thought it was awesome, and wanted to hire me on the spot. I had no idea what to charge, and I thought that $500 would be way too much to charge for coaching on a single piece of content. But they said yes without blinking an eye.
>
> I talked to another friend that afternoon and brought up the idea to her, and she too wanted to hire me! I again said I charged $500 for the project and she instantly said yes.

Over the next month or so, I tested the idea with my email list and I let everyone I knew know that I'd be doing some 1-on-1 coaching. I started getting more and more clients. I charged $1,000. Then $1,500. Then $4,000. And $5,000.

None of them blinked an eye at the price. The $5,000 client even told me a few weeks later that I should charge $10k or $20k for such a service if I work with established companies.

I was blown away."—Primoz B.

For some businesses, a $5 product makes sense. Maybe it makes sense for your business, and maybe not. That's something you need to decide for yourself. But my guess is that most of us don't want to play in the $5 sandbox, whether we're selling products or services. Typically, it's more fun (and profitable) to be a higher value provider. We're just held back by fear.

Most of Us Aren't Natural Salespeople

The fear of selling, fear of charging what you're worth, is totally normal. As you've seen, most entrepreneurs go through it. I struggled with it for a long time.

But when you nail the right audience, then as we like to say, "Price is a mere triviality." People will pay a substantial amount if you're actually solving a problem that's important to them AND they believe you can solve it.

That's the key to selling without feeling sleazy, so I'll say it again:

If you are solving a problem that's important to people, AND if you have the credibility so that they believe you can solve it, then price becomes a mere triviality.

Few people are natural-born salespeople, and honestly, that's okay. You don't need to be. But you do need to believe in what you sell. When you do, your customers will too, and they'll be happy to pay.

7. THE MAGIC OF BUILDING AUTOMATIC REVENUE INTO YOUR BUSINESS

You remember that $4.95 e-book I created back in 2007?

Well, check this out this email.

From: **Corbett** ▆▆▆▆ **via PayPal** <member@paypal.com>
Date: Mon, Dec 21, 2015 at 10:50 AM
Subject: Corbett ▆▆▆▆ just sent you $4.95 USD with PayPal.
To: Ramit Sethi <ramit@ramitsethi.com>

Hello Ramit Sethi,

Corbett ▆▆▆▆ just sent you money with PayPal.

Payment details

Amount: $4.95 USD

Transaction Date: December 21, 2015

Transaction ID: ▆▆▆▆▆▆

Message: Buying Ramit's 2007 Guide to Kicking Ass(▆▆▆▆-1) at Price: USD4.9500

What do you notice? YEARS after launching this product, I'm STILL generating income from it. Do you know how great it feels to get this email...over...and over...and over? Sure, it's less than $5, but imagine having a library of products. There are $200 products, the $497 products, the $997 ones, and on and on...

Sales happen automatically. I was not involved whatsoever—but my systems were. The right system is the linchpin that gives you total control over your life. Imagine waking up on a weekday, whenever you want.

You take your time getting up, brew some coffee, and check your email. And you see you received 10 sales...Most for $497, a couple for $997, and even one for $1,997...All while you were sleeping. This kind of revenue can be life changing.

Now forget about the $1,997 product, and even a $197 product for a second. What if you had an entry-level $50 product or service? Run this quick calculation in your head:

$50 product x 10 sales/month x 24 months = ?

Go ahead, take a second...

That's $12,000.

$12,000 in your pocket, JUST from an entry-level product, one sale every 3 days, and quitting after 2 years. Notice how conservative we're being. When I first started, my goal was to sell 2 products per day. Just 2, and I would have been thrilled.

Now, my goals are obviously much larger. But regardless of your goals, whether it's...

- 1 product every 3 days
- 2 products every 1 day
- Or 10 products every 1 day

…the same system can help you reach all those goals. I emphasize this because I invented my own systems, then spent years tweaking and perfecting them. Few others do, because it's easier to focus on tactical minutiae like "You must get on Twitter!" and "Use this life hack!" or "Optimize your opt-in form!"

But my students will tell you—systems are what allow you to go from an idea to a scalable, repeatable business that lets you help others while living the life you want:

> *"A year ago, if a stranger had sent me $500 in my email on a random Friday night, I would have flipped out. Now, it's becoming more common…My wife and I will be sitting around unwinding with a glass of wine and I will check my phone and I will say casually, 'Oh, hey, two people I've never met before just sent me $1,000.' It's still an awesome feeling, but incredibly, becoming more commonplace."*—John C.

> *"I'm doing over $10,000 per month when previously I thought in a good YEAR I might like to do $10,000. Overall, I feel less stress about finances. I used to wake up in the morning and kind of feel like I had to go, go, go. Having a growing business takes a lot of that stress and pressure off of me, knowing that you have this asset that's going to keep on allowing you to live your life without having to feel like you're in the rat race every single day."*—Bryce C.

> *"There were people who bought from me, and they emailed me to say, "We had never heard about you. We landed on your sales page, and we bought on the spot."*—Bushra A.

What Kind of Entrepreneur Do You Want to Be?

I think we can all agree: Life is messy.

My life is messy. I run a remote company of 50+ employees, flung all over the world. I also workout and squeeze in fun things to do in New York City on the weekends. I wish it all flowed seamlessly, but the truth is, it's *messy*! It's not like I'm sitting in front of this beautiful dashboard, flipping through tasks like *Minority Report*.

Some of my students run remote businesses like mine, and also live a remote lifestyle. They travel the globe while working out of whatever coffee shop has the best Wi-Fi. A fun, but messy, life.

Other students are parents—their lives are probably the most chaotic! 2 or 3 kids to shuttle to and from school, then off to swimming and soccer and ballet. They also work 9-5, make time to workout AND in their spare time, they're running a 6-figure business.

Life is always going to be messy. But the most successful people don't rely on "motivation" or "working harder" to get things done. Instead, they have systems for the big, big wins, and let the inconsequential stuff fall to the wayside. As your business gets increasingly successful and complex, this becomes more and more important.

You see, ultimately there are 2 types of entrepreneurs.

The first type is the one who's constantly complaining about feeling overwhelmed. We all know people like that. You ask them, "How are you doing today?" and you know exactly what you'll hear in response: "Really busy. Crazy busy." They look frazzled, like they can't believe how unfair life is.

Meanwhile, the second type, you ask them how everything's going, and they say, "Yeah, it's really good. Business is good." And you're just like, "Oh, okay." You wouldn't know if they were in the middle of their most complex campaign in their career, because everything's handled.

It's not natural skill or intelligence or work ethic that separates these 2 types of entrepreneurs. Just a systems mentality.

So far we've talked a lot about the math behind these systems, but I want to do more than show you some numbers. I actually want to walk you through how to start building your own systems. Let me show you a few of the first systems we developed, that we continue to use to this day, including our system for automating revenue.

System #1: Instant 10x Productivity

My friend asked me how I manage my to-dos. I pulled up my calendar and showed him how this system runs my life. If it's not on my calendar, it doesn't exist.

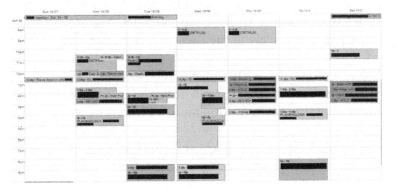

I even add random to-dos that I would normally put in the back of my head…and it would never get done. Instead, I add it to my calendar so it gets done.

Here are a couple advanced tips that make this super powerful: I set up weekly, monthly, and quarterly "to-dos" for things like reviewing my systems, planning strategy, even to find fun things to do in New York City.

I batch most of my meetings for the afternoon, but try to include at least a 5-minute buffer between them. I found when I stacked too many meetings in a row, I'd really lose my energy, and that's when bad things would start to happen.

Finally, within each task, I include the URLs of any necessary documents. I click the URL, and I'm instantly taken to the right place in the document—down to the paragraph I need to start working on.

You don't have to get to this level right now. This is just me being a weirdo, but at every single opportunity I'm looking for any place where I can cut inefficiency and just get to doing the works.

System #2: Generating Endless Ideas to Write About

Image grabbing your coffee, taking that first satisfying sip, then sitting down in front of the computer. You stretch your arms, put your fingers to the keyboard, then…nothing.

You've got no idea what to write. We call this "Blank Page Syndrome" and as any writer will attest, it's one of the most frustrating things to go through.

We decided we wanted to kill this problem once and for all. Let me show you our system to consistently come up with enough ideas to write blog posts, multiple emails, and high-end programs...over the last 10 years. It's a powerful yet surprisingly simple system that will generate an endless amount of ideas for years to come.

The magic lies in the first email in your email autoresponder. (If you don't have an email list or autoresponder set up yet, go to growthlab.com/your-move for resources on how to get started.) In this first email, you're going welcome them to your list, thank them for joining, and close with this question:

"What are you struggling with today?"

And when your potential customers start emailing you, telling you about their biggest pains, you have to email them back and dig deeper.

In Chapter 3: The secret to creating 100, 1,000, or 10,000 loyal customers, we talked about 3 questions to discover your customer's biggest hopes, fears, and dreams: What's going on? How do you think about this? How does it make you feel?

Some things you might hear:

- "I study a lot, but when I get the test, it's like everything falls out of my brain."
- "I run 2x per week and eat pretty healthy, but still can't fit into my favorite pair of jeans."
- "When I approach a girl, I just start rambling and sweating, I hate it."

People can't help but open up when you ask them these questions—and that'll provide you with the "gold" you need for blog posts, emails, and products your customers want.

System #3: Collect Raving Testimonials for Every Product

You may have noticed that with every course we launch we have raving testimonials: texts, graphics, video, and more. That's because we have a system for gathering, sorting, and deploying them. And once you start using testimonials strategically, they'll help your business grow in a huge way.

The key is: Do the work before you NEED it. It's like drinking water when you're thirsty—that means you already let your body get dehydrated. You'll want testimonials "in the can" BEFORE you start selling your first product.

First and foremost, let's assume your product or service is good (the world's best system won't save a terrible product or service). Next, we look for opportunities to ask for a testimonial *at every stage*:

At the start of a program, we ask, "Why'd you join?" During the program, we include surveys built right into the curriculum, or we may send out occasional emails. Then at the end of the course, we'll ask "How did it go? Where are you compared to where you expected? What could we do to improve?" We're looking to improve the product of course, but it's also a way to mine for amazing testimonials.

Don't overthink sorting your testimonials. For example, I used Gmail tags for years. You can use Gmail, Evernote or Google Docs, whatever's best for you. The key is, the system creates a virtuous cycle. The better your product is, the more testimonials you're going to get. The more testimonials you strategically use, the more people you're going to get in your program, and on and on and on.

System #4: Making Money While You Sleep

We've covered systems you can put to work TODAY that'll help you boost productivity and have an endless stream of content ideas.

Now, I want to show you the system that's the foundation for any business: our system for earning revenue, automatically. Remember our Rules of Money #3: Money is the marker you're doing the right thing. Without a properly set-up system for earning money, all your other business systems are purely for show.

Here's our system for automating revenue at a glance:

| READER VISITS YOUR SITE | SUBSCRIBES YOUR LIST | READS YOUR EMAILS | CLICKS TO YOUR SALES PAGE | BUYS YOUR PRODUCT |

As you can see, we keep it pretty simple: These 5 steps are enough to sell 20 different products across multiple industries, and generate millions of dollars. In fact, when you're just starting out, you really only need **3 components to get started**:

First, you need traffic. In other words, you need people coming to your website (or your store) who are interested in what you're selling. When it comes to traffic, the key takeaway is **quality over quantity.** You'd rather have 100 people who are desperate for your service, than 1,000 who are mildly interested.

Traffic is the lifeblood of your business—that means generally, the more traffic you have, the healthier your business. If you run an online business, this is pageviews. If you have a retail store like Zara, it's foot traffic.

Traffic also builds over time: The first day a restaurant opens, only a few people might stop in. But as word of great food, service, and value spreads, you're going to see that same restaurant packed every night. Which is why it's critical that each time you have a happy customer, you ask them to spread the message for you: Good people know good people.

Next, you need a product. And it has to be good! The world's best marketing and a never-ending flood of traffic can't save a shoddy product. That's why in the information products space, there are so many fly-by businesses that make A LOT of noise for a few months…then quietly disappear.

Building a great product takes work. A great product is based on what people actually want, not what some "expert" sitting up in his ivory tower thinks they need. We spend months, even years doing our research and developing our programs. While you don't have to spend that much time, you do have to listen to your customer.

Remember: great products don't rely on discounted prices. If you sold the world's greatest product at preventing hair loss or stopping acne, why would you discount? People would be happy to pay full price if it solved their problem once and for all.

Finally, you need a sales page. This is where you ask for the sale. In our business, we use sales pages. If you're a garage owner selling car services, this is your list of services, like tune-ups, tire rotations, and oil changes.

Some of our sales pages are over 70 pages long. A sales page doesn't need to be short! We spend 50-70% of the time really talking about the problem. We reveal their secret dreams and biggest pains, we talk about the other solutions available to them…and only then do we talk about our solution.

And when it's time to ask for the sale, we ask unapologetically. If your product or service really will solve their problem, whether it's finding a better job or finally getting out of debt, you have an obligation to do everything in your power to get them to buy.

Those are the 3 parts of our system for earning money automatically. As your products and offerings get more and more sophisticated, you'll be able to charge premium prices more frequently, which leads to results like this:

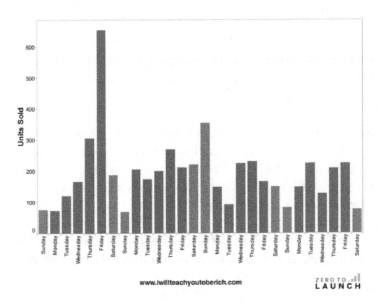

www.iwillteachyoutoberich.com

ZERO TO
LAUNCH

"I was able to deeply understand the types of people who would apply, what exactly they were looking for. They weren't actually looking to hear about certain things, like retainer models.

They wanted to understand, it's like, 'How did this guy, Naveen, build this system so that he doesn't have to do [work]? He makes revenue and it's not associated to time?'

I was able to use the right words, the positioning, the phrases, the language of my customers, in terms of what they desired, in order to help persuade them that the system was for them.

And in just a matter of a month—I don't even think it's been a month. I've had multiple people—multiple people!—interested (very interested) in it. And I've booked nearly $10,000 in online product revenue, and I don't even have a website."— Naveen D.

Focus On What Matters. Ignore Everything Else

You've just learned four systems you can use to be more productive and earn more money.

My friend, Sam Carpenter, literally wrote the book on systems called *Work the System*, and I love how he cuts right to the importance of systems. The important thing for any system, he says, isn't how complicated it is or how many moving parts there are or what technology it involves.

According to Sam, an effective system "focuses our limited attention and willpower on the things that matter."

No wonder why Sam and I are friends.

I loved this. I love anything that removes willpower, motivation, or passion from the equation…which is precisely what systems do. Systems don't care if you're excited about a new project or tired from a late night. Systems are impervious. They just keep working.

Once you get a system running properly, you continue to benefit from it forever. In my calendar example from before, you might save one hour a week. That's over 50 hours a year. Now imagine, you can optimize that, maybe save two or three hours per week. Soon we're talking about hundreds of hours of savings per year. That adds up to a lot.

More importantly, you can see how "systems thinking" doesn't just apply to your business. It applies to every part of your life. For example, hate coming home to an empty fridge after a long day of work? A simple system might be a grocery list you keep on the fridge. A more complicated system would involve paying someone to buy and deliver groceries to you every week.

> *"How do I handle the gym? I used to live a half mile from campus before I moved, what I said was, 'Oh, this is simple. The way I get to work is I run. I don't have a car. It's too long to walk, so I have to run to work. I bought a waterproof backpack and I can put a change of clothes in there.*
>
> *'Okay, well if I run to work, I'm going to be sweaty, so I have to get a locker at the gym so I can shower when I get there. Well, now that I'm at the gym and I've just done a run, well I'm might as well do a ten minute pull up based bodyweight workout. I'm there. I'm warmed up. It's the first thing in the morning. That's not really the worst thing to do, since I'm there and I'm going to have to take a shower anyway.'*

That turned out to be a wonderfully sustainable plan that gets me to the gym every day and had me working out every day in a very efficient way, because it was a system that made sense, and it was realistic with my energy levels. It was something that had all the pieces in place.

If I had just said, 'I need to go to the gym more. I have a gym membership. It's not far from my office. It's on campus. I need to go more.' Good luck, right? That's not a specific plan that realistically fits into my energy levels that I trust will work."—Cal Newport, author of *So Good They Can't Ignore You.*

You can apply systems to your business, your home, even your relationships (like an alarm, once a week, that reminds you to call your mom). It's not sexy, but it works.

Remember, I'm not saying you have to be a weirdo like I am about systems. You don't have to love them, and you certainly don't have to start documenting every process and every iota of your life. In fact, I recommend you start small—only document one or two processes at a time.

As you grow, you'll develop new, more complicated systems that help you focus more on what matters…so you can ignore everything else.

8. FIELD REPORT: HOW TO EARN $10,000 PER MONTH, EVEN IF YOU CAN'T SELL BY NAGINA ABDULLAH

Nagina Abdullah is a health coach for ambitious women. She built an online business that makes an extra 6 figures on the side of her day job, while raising 2 children.

I started my weight-loss blog, MasalaBody.com, as a hobby. I didn't even think about making money from it. I simply wanted to help other women feel like I did after losing 40 pounds: energized and confident.

Today, my site brings in more than $10,000/month—while I'm busy enjoying my full-time job and two kids. But before I could turn my blog into a profitable, automated business, I had to learn how to sell. And I hated selling.

I thought selling meant you had to scream at people in ALL CAPS. I didn't want to do that, so instead I barely sold at all! I might add a line at the very end of an email once in awhile.

The results: Some months I made a couple thousand dollars. But other months I made $0. These inconsistent sales weren't going to cut it. So I learned to overcome my fear of selling—and ended 2015 with four consecutive $10,000+ months.

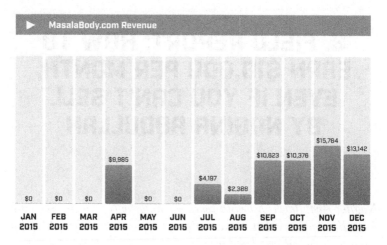

MasalaBody.com Revenue

	JAN 2015	FEB 2015	MAR 2015	APR 2015	MAY 2015	JUN 2015	JUL 2015	AUG 2015	SEP 2015	OCT 2015	NOV 2015	DEC 2015
	$0	$0	$0	$9,985	$0	$0	$4,197	$2,388	$10,623	$10,376	$15,764	$13,142

Total 2015 sales: $66,475—more than double 2014.

Here are a few of the things I did that took me from inconsistent sales to making more than $10K every month—and overcoming this fear of selling.

Get Inside Your Customers' Minds

If you want to sell with confidence, before you do anything else, you need to understand your customers like they are good friends. The reason is, you already know how to sell to your friends. You sell them on what TV show to watch next and what restaurant they absolutely need to try. And it's not sleazy. Part of that is because you have their best interest at heart. But it's also because you know them so well you can make valuable recommendations.

Selling to anyone involves the same building blocks. To sell, you need to know four key things about your customers: their hopes, dreams, pain points, and fears.

HOPES	What are their goals? What do they hope to achieve?
DREAMS	What will happen once they reach their goals? How will their life change?
PAIN POINTS	What challenges do they face? What is getting in the way of reaching their goal?
FEARS	What are they scared of if they don't achieve their dream?

There are three easy ways to get the answers to these questions: surveys, talking to your customers in person, and good old-fashioned research.

Surveys

Sending a survey to people in your target audience has two benefits. First, you'll get a lot of insights about what they're thinking. Second, you'll get the exact words to use in your copy so that your audience will listen to you.

Before you start writing questions, think about when you get a survey: What's the #1 thing that determines if you're going to answer it? Length, right? So why would you create a 15-question survey and think anyone will answer it?

I recommend 5 questions at the max. Make 2-3 of those open-ended. You learn so much more when people explain their answers instead of just selecting "Yes," "No," or "C." Also, that way you can capture the person's words and feelings.

Here are some questions that gave me amazing insights that'll work for you:

- What do you want for yourself [in specific topic]?
- What are you doing now? How does that make you feel?
- What's your alternative? How does that make you feel?

Surveys aren't fancy, but they work. It doesn't need to be complicated. Use a free survey tool like SurveyMonkey and move on. Then email the survey link to your friends or readers. You don't need hundreds of people to answer your survey. I sent mine to 40-50 people, and 15 completed it. In general, I expect a 20-30% response rate, which gives you a pretty good understanding of your audience.

Real-life Conversations

Surveys are valuable, but you also need to actually talk to your audience. You can learn as much from a 1-hour interview or conversation as you can from 100 survey responses and weeks of online research.

The key is to ask open-ended questions and let them talk. Take notes as they talk, or, if you have a good memory, record the conversation in a document after. You want their words—not your interpretation of them.

Be shameless. Start these conversations when you're with any-one in your target audience. For example, one day I went to drinks with 3 friends, and I started a discussion that went on for more than an hour.

I simply asked, "Are you able to control what you eat at night?" This is a pain point I discovered through other research, so I thought it would generate a lot of conversation.

And it did! My friends starting talking over each other about how they sneak to their kitchens at night to get peanut butter and chocolate. One even told me that she made her husband go buy Haagen Dazs Caramel Cone ice cream in the middle of the night.

After I left that night, I typed our conversation into the "Notes" app in my phone so I didn't forget anything. Later I did some research and discovered that the Caramel Cone flavor my friend couldn't stop talking about was the brand's #1 selling flavor!

So in a blog post, I called out this ice cream and talked about how, even though we try to control ourselves, something hap-pens at night that removes all logic. People loved this email! People sent me replies saying, "It's like you're reading my mind" and "I relate to your stories so much!"

Use the notes from your conversations in the same way. When you notice that a certain word or phrase keeps popping up, use that in a blog post, in an email, or on your website.

This level of detail makes your readers feel like you under-stand exactly what they're going through. And that's far more influential than any facts or data you could provide.

One last note: If you can't think of anyone to talk to, look for Facebook groups that match your target audience. Then reach out to people in those groups to ask about chatting with them.

Internet Research

Though it's not as personal as surveys and interviews, you can learn a tremendous amount about your target audience with online research.

You want to look for the same four things you ask about in surveys or in-person conversations: their hopes, dreams, pain points, and fears. Again, look for overall topics that keep appearing and also document the exact words and phrases you see over and over.

Here are some of my top places to learn about your audience:

- Amazon reviews of similar products and books
- Reddit or other online posting sites
- Facebook groups

(For Amazon in particular, Tim Ferriss recommends that you read 3- and 4-star reviews, as those have the most insight about what the reviewer liked and didn't like.)

It's helpful to record these reviews in something like an Excel document and highlight the key terms you see and want to remember. Then everything is in one place, and the most important phrases stand out. This is exactly the type of research I used to develop my first product.

It started out as a $9.99 e-book. But after doing online research, I found that people said that they needed more tactical information to help them eat healthy. They didn't only want recipes, they also wanted menu plans and grocery lists. So instead, I sold a $5,000 premium coaching product. Although I had only a very basic website, I made my first $10,000 a month after launching.

Become a Master Storyteller

You've gathered all this great data. Now it's time to use it to tell stories. Storytelling is proven to help people learn and remember information.

The key is to hook readers from the start with a surprising or interesting statement. Then throughout your story, speak to readers in their language, and address their hopes, dreams, and fears.

You can tell the stories that you capture from others through your research. Or you can share your own stories about those same experiences. For example, since I live near New York City, I often heard women talk about feeling out of breath when they climb the subway stairs. They said this trigger makes them wish they weighed less and had more energy.

After a recent trip with my daughter on the subway, I noticed how energetic and light I felt as I walked up the stairs. I wrote about that trip as an inspirational story. I compared how I used to feel and how I feel now that I'm 40 pounds lighter. I wrote every sentence with my ideal clients' pain points and dreams in mind. I knew that the way I felt is how my target audience wants to feel.

At the end of this email, I offered my coaching program to help women feel the same way.

The result? $4,000 in sales from just this email. One of my new clients even told me that she decided to work with me because the story about walking up the subway stairs resonated with her!

Focus on "Why," Not "How"

The final change in selling my services was to stop writing about the "how" and instead write about the "why." Here's my first sales page from 3 years ago. See how much I focused on the "how":

> Do you want or need to lose weight but don't have time to go to the gym for hours everyday? Do you try to eat healthy but the food you eat is too boring and bland?
>
> Would you believe you could lose 10 pounds in one month by eating flavorful food? The KEY to losing weight FAST and KEEPING IT OFF is to like what you are eating, and eat the RIGHT things. By eating food that is efficient and gives you the energy and nutrients you need, you WILL lose weight.
>
> With a few basic spices and EXTREMELY easy cooking methods, food tastes flavorful and delicious.
>
> By adding spices and flavor to low-sugar foods, you will maintain a low-sugar blood level, you will enjoy what you eat, your weight will drop.
>
> What are some of these low-sugar foods? They include vegetables, proteins, beans and lentils. These foods are not only low in sugar, but they contain other ingredients that work with your body to make you feel full and to give you energy for a long time. Lentils and beans are full of fiber and "slow-burning carbohydrates" which give you energy for a long period of time, rather than a lot

No wonder people weren't buying.

The writing is almost like a science lesson. Yes, flavors and low-sugar foods help you lose weight. But this is not what convinces people to take action to lose weight.

When you focus on why someone wants something—what's driving them to go after their goal—you persuade them that it's worth changing. And that makes them more likely to give your solution (i.e. your product) a shot in helping them change.

Here's part of my sales page today. You'll see I talk about why people want to lose weight. These points are all based on the research I did.

- **Look and feel sexy** every time you look in the mirror
- **Slip into your jeans** comfortably
- **Feel the stare** from your husband or partner when you walk into a room
- **Surprise everyone** at your next reunion, wedding or holiday party because you look so fit and lean
- **Quickly get the energy** to take your kids or family hiking and climb to the top with your arms in the air saying, "YEAH! I DID IT!"

Craft your sales page like this, and—because you talk about your readers' wishes—they will likely click to learn more about your products. My page helps generate more than $10,000 every month now.

You Can Sell, Too—Without Being Sleazy

You don't need to scream at people in ALL CAPS or tell them to "act now!" to sell online.

Genuine selling starts with truly understanding the needs of your clients through surveys, conversations, and online research. Then you use that research to write engaging, inspiring stories. Lastly, you address why your clients want to change so they're motivated to take action.

This is a formula for running your business for the long game. Once you can make your readers feel like a friend, grab their attention, and inspire them, they'll crave more content and also the products you have to offer.

Want to see more of Nagina's story? Check out growthlab.com/your-move for a deeper look at her business and journey.

PART 3: GROWTH FOR TOMORROW

It's funny. Growing up as an Indian kid, I was a champion speller (of course). How did I get to be so good? I used to think it was that my mom would practice with me every day for hours.

That's partially true.

But the real reason I got so good is that she constantly challenged me with harder and harder words. It sounds obvious, but it's not.

This is what's called "deliberate practice" in that famous study of 10,000 hours to mastery.

It's also called "progressive overload" in fitness, where you constantly push yourself to more and more weight.

You and I intuitively get that this is a good thing. Yet isn't it surprising that most of us don't do it?

We take the same route to work each day.

We run for the same amount of time on the treadmill at the same speed.

We read the same sites and books, not challenging ourselves to read harder and denser ones.

I'm guilty of this, too. In college, I worked out for 6 months and used the exact same weights. No wonder I saw no changes.

It was only when I had a trainer show me about progressive overload that I realized—ahhh! This is why I got so good at spelling...and why I haven't budged in working out.

In this section on growth, I'm going to give you progressively more and more difficult challenges. At first, you may start off doing individual tasks, like having 1-on-1 conversations for customer research. DO NOT SKIP THESE! It's tempting to skip ahead to the sexy stuff, but just as you wouldn't walk into a gym and bench-press 225lbs, you shouldn't skip ahead without building a solid foundation.

Eventually, you'll hit a ceiling. That's normal. There are only so many insights you can get from 1-1 conversations if you want scale. We'll show you how to think about growth in this section.

9. GETTING STUCK IS NORMAL, BUT WINNERS GROW ANYWAY

Earlier this year I had one of the proudest moments of my career: I flew my entire team (100% remote) to an in-person meeting in Austin, Texas.

Besides all the sweet wildlife we saw, it was the latest step in the growth of IWT, which I started in my dorm room at Stanford. And now, look at this! It's insane!

There are plenty of articles written for the guy on the left. Let's call him Dorm Room Ramit. Dorm Room Ramit was a one-man "business" that didn't sell anything. He also was severely calorically undernourished. But what about after that? How did I get to the guy on the right, CEO Ramit? (I'm in the back.)

What changes between 1 employee and dozens? What happens when "beginner" advice isn't enough? What happens when you have more tasks than hours in the day and you have to prioritize?

You have to rethink everything.

As I built IWT over the course of a decade, I found myself having to reinvent my core principles, and it's something no one ever talks about.

After 13 years running IWT, here are 5 subtle but important things I changed my mind about as we grew.

Dorm Room Ramit: Everything Needs to be Perfect
CEO Ramit: Live to Fight Another Day

At the start of your business (anywhere from 0 to $100K revenue/year), every day you're fighting to live another day. You have to be scrappy. It's a game of survival, not perfection.

When I first started blogging, my site design was horrible. Everyone and their mother had an opinion on the color scheme, my headshot, and the font size. In the market, we were starting to see these beautiful "Web 2.0" websites, and I remember thinking "I want that," and feeling like I was missing out because my site wasn't PERFECT. And to be honest, it kept me down and unmotivated at times.

What I didn't realize at the time was that my lack of money was a blessing. Any wrong choice was at least an INEXPENSIVE wrong choice. And that let me fight another day. I also wanted sophisticated tools so I could properly segment my list, and elegantly drop readers into the perfect email funnel for them. But I didn't know how, and I couldn't afford new software, either.

Instead, I bought a very basic newsletter tool, mostly used by bloggers. It wasn't pretty—in fact, we set it up in this hack-y way because that's all I knew how to do. We stuck with it for years, until we were practically bursting at the seams.

Years later, it would cost us lots of money to fix that in our next software upgrade. We incurred a ton of technical debt. But at least by that point, we had the money and the people to fix it.

If we had tried to be perfect to begin with, we would have been dead.

When you cling to the idea of these things you want (but can't have yet), the tension gets to you. You become myopic about the work you're doing:

- "Oh, I can't start writing anything until I have a beautifully designed website."

- "I can't invite people to join my email list until I've written out a 15 email auto-responder."
- "I shouldn't do any guest posting until I have the perfectly optimized catcher's mitt."

Instead, we have to get comfortable with the idea of creating something imperfect. In the beginning, you can't spend time A/B testing your email headlines. You need to find out if people will buy in the first place.

Too many entrepreneurs worry about stuff they don't need to. They think they need to read books by Warren Buffett, master Evergreen launches, and build an affiliate program before they've successfully sold their first product.

Not that the advanced stuff doesn't matter. It does. But first…

Live to fight another day, and trust that your future self will be able to solve problems later on.

Dorm Room Ramit: A Popular Blog is a Business
CEO Ramit: A Profitable Blog is a Business

This one I wish I framed and put above my desk when I first started the blog.

For the first year, I was so afraid of what people would say if I tried to make ANY money, I didn't try ANYTHING. I didn't even create an email list. It was enough to have the appearance of a business at first. But eventually, I had to come to terms with the fact that I wasn't running a charity.

And neither are you.

But when I finally decided it was time to sell, I basically apologized profusely for charging the astronomical price of $4.95 for my first e-book.

Too many business owners track every vanity metric under the sun—visits, time on page, followers—because it feels nice to watch those numbers go up. That's for beginners looking for any motivation to stay at it. I get it.

Meanwhile, they completely ignore the ONE metric that actually matters: Profit.

Time-on-site won't pay your rent.

Remember Rule #3: Money is the marker that you're doing the right thing because money is the ultimate value to people. When someone is willing to open their wallet and give you their credit card—they value you enough to actually pay—then you know you're doing something to change their lives.

And when the money starts coming in, you can use it to solve most of your other "beginner" problems.

- Too many customer emails? Now you can hire the world's best customer service manager.
- Ugly headshots? Go buy new ones.
- Having issues with serving private video? Now you can pay $15,000 a year hosting your videos on the world's best platform.

Of course, we're not saying you have to charge on Day 1 of your business or that interaction with your customers needs to be transactional. Sometimes, you just want to do it for the likes.

But you have to be honest with yourself. If this is your business, then treat it like a business. And successful businesses need to be profitable.

Dorm Room Ramit: Be Good at Everything
CEO Ramit: Be World Class at a Few Things

When you start your company everything falls to you. You must know a little bit of everything to get the ball rolling. But eventually...it's time to focus.

The world does not reward jacks-of-all-trades. We're better off becoming really good at a few things. For example, early on I was writing blog posts, answering 100+ customer service emails, working directly with my friend (who was lending me his engineering skills), thinking about the logo design, and on and on.

I'm not good at most of that stuff!

I had a hard lesson to learn: Instead of becoming world class at customer service, and design, and engineering, and optimization (and on and on)...I really needed to become world class at building a team. The rest would fall into place.

Here's what I chose to become really good at:

- Writing
- Cracking the code on why people do what they do
- Understanding how to create products that people want—and products that get real results

That's it! For anyone starting out today, here are the three things I recommend you become world class at:

- Learning how to sell
- Writing amazing emails or blog posts that people open and read
- Learning how to build a team (even a small one)

Beware of choosing the wrong goals. If you choose the wrong things, even when you win, you lose. Case in point:

- Becoming someone who's excellent at reaching inbox zero. Who cares?
- Focusing solely on a technical skill like Excel analysis, but never learning to build relationships and work with others.
- Getting the coolest design on your blog. So what?

Dorm Room Ramit: I Don't Want to Hire a Big Team
CEO Ramit: I Want to Reach Millions of People

I don't know why, but I used to constantly say:

"I don't want a big team. I'd prefer to keep it small and intimate."

Did I know anything about the differences between large vs. small teams? No. Did I understand anything about managing a growing team, hiring, recruiting, retention, human resources, etc.? No. But I said it anyway.

Man, that was dumb.

Looking back, here's what I was actually saying:

- "I don't know how to build a team."
- "It's scary and it seems like a lot of work."

- "So I think I better say 'I don't want to do it.' That way I have an explanation for why I'm not doing it."

There's only one problem...I wanted to reach millions of people. I couldn't do that alone. Nobody can. So I had two choices: Cut my goals of reaching millions of people (not gonna happen)...or learn to build a team. I decided to learn to build a team.

We all tell ourselves stories. We've created narratives of our lives, some of them so deep, they're actually invisible scripts that guide our decisions and we don't even know it. We can change most of these narratives, but it takes a lot of work.

Dorm Room Ramit: I'll Only Follow "Timeless Principles"
CEO Ramit: What Got You Here Won't Get You There

It's comforting to think that if you find the right 2-3 "timeless principles," you can build an entire company around them. You know, things like "put the customer first" or "quality matters."

Wrong. Well, incomplete. Principles like that matter. But I realized I'd been operating under the assumption that if I just picked the right 2-3 principles, I could use them forever. What I didn't realize is that most of your days will be spent in gray areas. Should you build Product A or Product B? Can you afford to hire John? Uh oh, I don't know how to grow my business any more.

A better assumption: What got you here won't get you there (also the title of a great book by my friend, Marshall Goldsmith).

The things that worked from $0 to $100,000 won't always work when you're trying to crack $500,000. They certainly won't work at $5 million. Therefore, you have to get comfortable being uncomfortable. This is really, really hard.

For example, guest posting was something that worked great for us to get traffic...in the first few years. Getting on sites like Yahoo.com, The New York Times, and a handful of other blogs helped grow our email list.

Imagine writing an amazing guest post and getting 2,000 subscribers. If you have 50,000 subscribers, you just grew 4% overnight!

But now imagine that you have 300,000 subscribers. You put the same amount of time into writing an amazing guest post, and you get good results: another 2,000 subscribers. But this time, it only grew your list by 0.67%.

You can see how certain techniques become relatively ineffective over time. We continue to do it, but we've also invested into scalable SEO strategies—something I NEVER considered when I began.

Another example: When it came to video, I used to be able to just wing it if we were creating something for our YouTube channel or on a friend's blog. You can go check out my early YouTube clips. But when I started going onto national television, I knew it was critical to invest in a trainer, because my skills alone wouldn't get me to the next level.

Here are some of the challenges we're facing today. They helped get us this far, but as CEO, I'm learning they may be holding the company back from getting to the next level:

- **Remote work**. Working remotely is amazing...until you see how much amazing work your team can do when everyone is working under the same roof.
- **Writing product launches from scratch**. Writing fresh launches is great...until you're faced with the daunting task of writing 10-20 of them in a year.
- **"*I Will Teach You to Be Rich*."** IWTYTBR is a fine name. There's a lot of powerful brand awareness around it, until you're trying to recruit a new employee who doesn't know your story.

Does this mean that starting tomorrow, we're going to ditch the name "*I Will Teach You To Be Rich*"? Probably not, but you never know. What got you here won't get you there.

Looking Back on Dorm Room Ramit

Looking back now, I had some pretty dumb ideas about how business really worked. I hoped that I could read a few books, write down a few key principles, and then magically grow my business. Oh, and all without hiring anybody and without changing my playbook.

The biggest lesson I learned was to get comfortable with discomfort. It's really uncomfortable learning how to get your first customer. Then one day you realize, "Hey, I know how to do this."

This is the decision point. You can keep running that same playbook, and getting one customer after another...

...or you can say, "I know how to do this—what's next?" and begin working on strategies to get your next 10 customers. Then 100. Then 10,000.

That involves things you might not have ever considered, like hiring, corporate finance, and engineering management. All those things are outside the scope of this book, but that's really not the point.

The point is, the key to growth is looking into your own narratives and mastering your inner psychology.

How Olympians Train

What's the difference between top performers at the very highest levels?

Think about Olympians. What's the difference from one world-class runner to another? They both have similar genetic make-up. They both work hours and hours a day at their respective sports. What's the difference? What separates the gold medalists from the person who doesn't make it onto the podium?

Let me give you an example: When these runners start off at a very young age, there are vastly different skill levels. It's just how it is: You've got the fast guy in the class and the slow guy. Let's say you're really good. As you get more and more advanced, the people who are not good, they get weeded out and they just stop.

Now you've got a group of intermediate people, and the difference becomes relatively smaller. There aren't crazy differences, but it's like this: As you get to the more and more advanced levels, the differences in technical skill become almost negligible. At the very highest levels, the differences in technical skills have been virtually extinguished because all the people who are not amazing are out of the game; they're not competing at those levels.

In other words, at a certain point, we all have similar skill sets. You start off and some people are way better than others. Over time you work a little bit harder. Some people get weeded out because they're not good. But once you get to a certain level, basically people have similar skill sets. What's the difference, then?

It's the psychology that separates the winners from everyone else.

And I think the same is true in business. It's our psychology holding us back as the "Dorm Room" version of ourselves... and stopping us from reaching our "CEO" version.

But when we master this part of our psychology—I call this the psychology of growth—it's like we've been running with a heavy weight vest on, and now we've taken it off. Suddenly, you feel like you're flying. Every movement feels light, almost effortless.

There are a lot of different concepts to unlock our psychology. Here are the key concepts that helped me grow my business past the $100,000 revenue/year game, to the $1,000,000 game, and beyond.

Playing to Win

Playing to win means different things to different people.

For some of us, it means applying for different things that are maybe just slightly out of our reach. It may be applying for work with a Fortune 500 client that you're technically not qualified to work for. Even though you probably won't get it, you may learn something very, very significant in your research.

It may mean setting much bolder goals for your business. For example, let's say you're studying your competition. You notice you charge $60 an hour and they're charging $80. You're like, "How do they do it? How do they get away with that?"

My question is: Why are you even worrying about them, your competitors who charge $80? Why even bother? When I look for people to learn from, I don't look to businesses the same size as me—I want to look bigger! I study Wal-Mart, Costco, Louis Vuitton, Amazon, and other companies with a much bigger footprint than ours.

Most people don't set goals. When they do, the goals are so dim it's like a dying star. Instead of saying, "My goal is to increase revenue 10% per year," why not say, "My goal is to double it"? What would that do?

First, that competitor charging $80? No longer in your orbit. They're irrelevant to you. There's no point in comparing ourselves to someone who's only marginally better, when we could look 5 steps ahead and study what the best are doing.

I asked my friend, Derek Halpern from Social Triggers about this once. I asked him does he compare himself to others:

> "*I actually love to compare myself to other people. A lot of people might be demotivated by that. But it fires me up.*
>
> "*In 2006 or 2007, I had a goal of hitting six figures. Once I hit six figures, like the last four months of the year I did nothing.*

"Now, what I like to do is compare myself to others who are way ahead of me. And I find that having that kind of stretch goal is a way to keep me motivated to keep going towards what I want to go to."

When you set audacious goals, like doubling your revenue instead of increasing it by 10%, it gives your business instant clarity. You can immediately clear off your plate all the projects that won't help you reach the goal. "Is that going to help me double my revenue? If no, then kill it."

I've done this with many projects. We'll have a strategy call where we evaluate a product and study projected revenues. Looking at the numbers, it's easy to say, "There's no way that this is going to get us where we need to go. Kill the project," and it's killed that day.

If I'm playing to win, it's easy to make that decision. It doesn't matter if I really like the project, or if we're already 20% or 50% or 70% of the way to completion. If the best-case scenario is not helping me reach my goal, then I can kill it instantly and not lose any sleep over it.

When To Go "All In"

When starting a new project, most people hedge their bets. They say things like, "We'll see how it goes. I'm going to just throw this and see if it sticks." There's a certain point where this makes sense.

For example, when we put together our course called *Find Your Dream Job*, we didn't know what course we were going to build. There was a ton of research to sift through. We had a hundred thousand data points.

But once we narrowed it down and figured out, "This is it," we went all-in. We spared no expense: We brought in the right people to help us build and sell the program, we flew in students, we bought every book, and we tested it. We threw away our first 16 versions until we had it right.

This is what I mean by "Putting wood behind the arrow." It means if you're going to go all-in, go all-in.

You don't have to go all-in on everything—in fact, you shouldn't. Instead aim for 3 to 5 things per year to move all-in on—things that take 100% of your time, money, and attention. We pick those 3 to 5 things carefully, and once they're picked, we expect success. We might not always win, but we play to win.

For example, years back we launched a course. We thought it was very good. We knew the content helped a lot of students in the past, so we repackaged it into a new course. We launched—and it completely bombed.

Not only that, people were refunding with the first couple hours of buying it! That never happens. So we pulled the program and dove back into the research. We discovered several subtle insights that we had missed, very subtle things in the marketing.

We fixed them and improved the marketing. I did another webcast and didn't change a word on the slides. The first webcast we generated a 3% conversion: so out of 100 people, 3 joined the program.

On the next one, with identical slides, we converted at 26%—a jump in 23% without even touching the product.

We could only do this because we "Played to win," and "Put wood behind our arrows." We released something we realized wasn't our best. But because we expect success, we went back and fixed it.

No one can expect to win every time, but we're always going to try for it.

Commit to Professionalism

This is not something I typically talk about publicly, but it's something that we do implicitly, explicitly, and we've done it more and more as we've grown. And it's dripped down to every other part of our business.

My first videos were in my San Francisco apartment, on my laptop. They're just not that professional, but it was fine. I was really skinny and I was in a Superman t-shirt, and I'm telling you how to do asset allocation.

People liked it and it was authentic, but now you see the videos and you'd think: "What? Who is this dude?" Today, our videos are shot in a beautiful studio, people actually wear collared shirts, and it's all very professional.

The videos are still fun. I'm still telling jokes, I still rant about the stupid questions I get. But you can tell the professionalism has moved up a little bit. The personality is still there—it's not like I became some stuffy old man, but it's just a little higher quality.

Professionalism is a concept a lot of businesses gloss over—especially when they're starting out and people think it's okay to wear flip flops to a meeting because that's what Mark Zuckerberg did. You're not Mark Zuckerberg.

I spoke at a conference for online marketers, and was sharing some of the growth strategies that have worked for us. Afterward, 5 people came up to me separately and said, "Thank you for dressing up in a suit and thank you for being professional."

At the time I thought it was really unusual, but thinking about this conference, it made perfect sense. The other speakers presented in t-shirts and jeans, and worked off of slide decks they just threw together.

When you go to an I Will Teach event, you better believe it's going to be professional: From the website, to the emails, to the second you get to the event. You're going to be taken care of. It's like ordering from Amazon—you know your order is going to be handled. That professionalism gives all of your customers confidence.

Here are more examples of communicating professionalism:

Number 1: Being 100% prepared.

When I coordinated with our event planner to do a top-to-bottom review of an event, she had a list of things to go down. She gets down to Number 3, and I just cut in. I start asking my own questions. I'm like, "What about this? What about that?"

A ton of random questions, and she answers every one. That's professional.

At any I Will Teach meeting, the agenda is sent out beforehand, and every action item is laid out. If there's a question for a Product Developer or a UX Designer, their name is in capitals and it's highlighted. We know exactly who's on the call because they bold themselves. It's all done, so we can jump right into the action items. That's being 100% prepared. Anyone who comes into an IWT meeting from the outside is SHOCKED at this level of preparation.

Number 2: Being proactive

It's really easy to go into a client meeting, listen to what they want, and do it. It's easy to send out an email with some newsletter tool, then never follow-up with any of your readers. This is table stakes.

What would be amazing is to go in there and say, "Last week you wanted me to deliver X. Here it is. Also, I noticed there's something else that you mentioned you were interested in. I've actually done some work on that over here—take a look."

They already trust you to work on one thing—now they're more likely to trust you with MORE responsibility. That's being proactive.

Or what about sending a weekly report? If your business serves busy people, I'm talking about 6-figure, 7-figure clients, they don't have time to get into your details of "did you check the code on this or that?" They don't care. They just want the weekly update:

"What did you say you were going to do? What did you do? What are the roadblocks?"

Being proactive goes a LONG way in committing to professionalism.

Number 3: Teach them to revere your work

Years ago, I did an hour-long interview with one of my mentors. It took 16 hours of research before we ever sat down—and I gave it to my readers for free. But I included this caveat:

"Treat it like something you spent $1,000 on. Use it. Implement it. Don't just listen to it and then move on with your life. There are dozens of profoundly useful and applicable techniques that you can use to kick-start a project, get out of a rut, improve your health, make more money, improve your relationships, excel at work, and challenge your beliefs about behavioral change."

Why did I include that?

Because as a professional, it's your job to teach them—your clients, customers, and team—to revere your work. If you don't, then they won't respect the work you do. It's that simple.

A friend of mine used to sell low-cost information products, in the $29 range, and he wanted to move upmarket, to $1,000 products. He asks, "Can you help me take a look at my sales page?"

"Sure," I said. "I'll give you feedback on your sales page, but you have to send me the notes that you take from our call." Why did I do that?

The guy's my friend, I'm not going to charge him to look at his sales page, but my work is highly valuable and I teach everyone to revere it. That is my goal. By telling him, "I want you to send me the notes on our call," I'm teaching him 2 things:

1. This is going to be so valuable that you're going to want to take notes. I want him to understand that message.
2. Those notes are going to be so valuable that **I'm going to want to use them too.** I'm going to save them, file them away, and one day if I create something on sales page critiques, I have my notes.

Notice the messaging in both of these examples. I'm polite but firm. I'm communicating my value. That's professionalism.

One Year From Now Where Will You Be?

There are no 1-2-3 action steps for mastering the psychology of growth. These are things that we try to change on a day-to-day basis. We commit to them, and use them as a guideline for our decisions.

For example, let's say it's late at night, and a client emails you. Do you respond? In your business, what would a professional do? There's no one right answer. You have to decide for yourself: What do your customers, clients, and employees expect? Then, act accordingly.

Apply these concepts every day, and they will transform your business a year from now. A year from now, you'll look back and see you've tripled your revenue, or you've doubled your customer base, or you took a long vacation while your business continued to hum along. You won't believe how much you've grown.

10. FINDING A MENTOR: HOW TO SUPERCHARGE YOUR SUCCESS

I have a lot of mentors. They've made a huge impact on my education and career. They've played a huge role in taking me from where I began, and helping me amplify my results.

It's almost like having mentors supercharged me to get where I was going FASTER, and also course-correcting me if I made wrong decisions along the way.

What I took away from those mentors continues to affect my business today.

For example, I learned from Seth Godin that while it takes 2x or 3x the amount of work to become the absolute best in your field, the best reap 5x or 10x the reward as everyone else. I call this "disproportionate results."

Seth Godin is one of the master storytellers and marketers of his time. Because he's the best, he no longer needs to spend time hunting down interesting stories or anecdotes. Instead, people just send them to him, hundreds every week. Seth gets to handpick the very best.

Another mentor is BJ Fogg, the director at Stanford's persuasive technology lab. BJ taught me the skills that are the foundation to my business: writing effective emails, how to run meetings, and the deep theoretical knowledge of how to change behavior.

Finally, Jay Abraham's insights completely changed my life. His book made me over $100,000 in one month, and he helped me double my business in one year. I applied his advice to my personal life and had amazing experiences in just a few months.

So whether you're starting a business or not, I think everyone would benefit from a mentor. I think of my mentors almost like my secret weapons. If I have a question I'm not sure about: a piece of business strategy, or "Should I do this deal?" or "Is this even the right path to go on?" I make one phone call and get amazing clarity.

You'd think everyone would want this, right? However, when I started doing the research, I discovered something interesting. I found that many people claim they want a mentor…but they don't actually want to put in the work to get one!

They want the results, the option to call someone up with a ton of experience and ask a question…but they don't actually want to cultivate and develop that relationship.

Now, if you're reading this book, you probably understand the value of having a great mentor, and you're willing to put in the work to develop that relationship.

Let me share one of my favorite stories about finding a mentor. This was posted by Ravi Mohan, a director of a VC firm. It'll show you how most people approach finding a mentor, compared to how Ravi did it:

> *"Once upon a time I was in a situation where I thought I could contribute to something one of the best programmers in the world was working on.*

"*I sent an email that said something to the effect of 'You say on this webpage you need this code and I have been working on something similar in my spare time and I could write the rest for you over the next few months because I am interested in what you are doing.'*"

"*I got a 2 line reply which said something like, 'A lot of people write to me saying they'll do this, but I've never seen any code yet so I am a little skeptical. Don't take it personally. Thanks. Bye.'*"

A little bit off-putting, but I definitely understand this busy guy's response. I get things like that all the time. People email, "Hey can you give me answers to these questions?" that, by the way, I've already answered 6 million times.

Ravi continues:

"*So in the next email (sent a minute after I received his reply) I sent him a zipped file of code with an explanation that 'This is what I've done so far which is about 70% of what you want.'*"

"*He immediately replied saying 'Whoa you are serious. That is refreshing...' and opened up completely, giving me a lot of useful feedback and very specific advice. He is a very valued mentor to this day.*"

"*In other words, when you ask for a busy person's time for mentorship or advice, show that (1) You're serious and you've gone as far as you can by yourself, and (2) You've taken concrete steps to address whatever your needs are, and show how you can benefit them and their project.*"

Compare this to the usual email I get, probably 5 to 10x a day: "Can you mentor me?" No one who's serious ever asks, "Can you mentor me?"

That's like me going to a bar, and going up to a random girl, "Will you hook up with me?" Do you ever say those words? No! You use different language. You have a whole different process, because you want to build a relationship!

You don't just go in there and say, "Hey, I have these 58 questions about conversion optimization and email automation and oh by the way, will you become my mentor?"

The answer isn't even a "no." It's a "delete." Think about that.

Most of us, when we look for a mentor, we approach someone we've been following, and we don't know what to do. So we just go crazy and shout, "Yeah! Please become my mentor!"

In reality, the first thing isn't asking. The first thing is figuring out how you can help THEM.

Don't Ask for Anything
Charlie Hoehn has worked for me, Tucker Max, and Tim Ferriss. I asked for his biggest insights into landing big-name mentors like this.

One of the things he shared was: If you want to befriend a really busy, famous person, the first thing you do is you DON'T ASK THEM FOR ANYTHING.

These people are surrounded by people who want something from them! Hundreds, sometimes even thousands of people.

What if you could just offer something, without asking for anything?

Do you think you would stand out?

"I Made it all Upside for Him"

Ryan Holiday is an author, newspaper editor, and was a Director of Marketing at American Apparel. When he was in college, he wrote a column for his newspaper, and he decided he'd use the column to reach out to people he wanted to connect with.

So, he reviewed Tucker Max's website. The genius of this is that everyone likes to be reviewed, especially early in their career.

Unlike everyone else that dismissed Tucker, Ryan wrote about his site in a deep, appreciative, (but not fawning) kind of way. Then he sent him the article, and the connection was made.

Ryan stayed in touch for months, looking for any excuse to email him that wasn't bothersome. For example, he'd write, "Hey, I read this article, thought maybe you would like it. Let me know what you think?"

Ryan spent a lot of time just creating rapport, and slowly would do research on things Tucker wanted. Eventually, they got coffee in New York City, and Ryan pitched him:

"I noticed he had a bunch of unsold advertising inventory. I had some idea with what he could do with it. I said, 'I'm not asking you to pay me, I'm not asking for a hand-out, and I'm not asking you to take me under your wing. Let me try this, and if it works, awesome.'

"It didn't end up working out. But the point is, I took some initiative, I had a real tangible suggestion that was basically all upside for him, and I worked hard and was reliable. The next time he had something he needed someone to do, I was the person he asked."

Good, Old-Fashioned Hard Work

Before Sheryl Sandberg's name became synonymous with Facebook and the "Lean In" movement, her determination and honesty already attracted the mentorship of Larry Summers.

When Sheryl was a junior at Harvard, she formed a new student organization encouraging women to major in Economics and Government. Larry not only rallied the support of the Harvard professors for this organization, he also went on to be Sheryl's advisor for her senior Economics thesis.

"Sheryl always believed that if there were 30 things on her to-do list at the beginning of the day, there would be 30 check marks at the end of the day," Larry said in an interview with The Guardian. When he became chief economist at the World Bank, he recruited Sheryl as a research assistant.

He later became Treasury Secretary in the Clinton administration. Sheryl was quickly appointed as his Chief of Staff. What made her such an asset?

"If I was making a mistake, she told me." Larry said. "She was totally loyal, but totally in my face."

You've seen how finding the right mentor can put your business, career, and personal development on a rocket ship. Now, let's talk about how you attract mentors.

Do Your Homework

Busy, important people LOVE helping others who take action.

Now, here's some good news: Most people are pretty terrible at taking action! So if you're even slightly better than the average, you can easily stand out from amongst the masses. For example, when others reach out to a busy person, usually they word vomit their autobiography into one run-on sentence, realize what they did, and wrap up by saying, "So, uh…hope to hear back from you." And they get ignored.

Why would the busy person respond to them when they haven't done the homework to be able to write a succinct email? Similarly, if you are asking stupid questions like "How do you get the motivation to accomplish so much?" plan on being ignored. If you want someone to sing Kumbaya to you, find a vegan non-profit employee. If you want a mentor, DO YOUR HOMEWORK.

What does doing your homework look like?

It means really going deep in the archives and reading every blog post they've ever written. It means following them on Twitter, Facebook, and Instagram to get an idea about what they're passionate about. Then, watching every YouTube video they've posted on their channel.

So when it's time to send that email, you can use what I call the "1-2-3 Choice Technique." The email says something like this:

"Hi Ramit, I love your book on blah blah.

I noticed you said I should XYZ in chapter 5, and so I tried it. I'm stuck due to XYZ. So I've come up with 3 possible routes:

Option 1

Option 2

Option 3

Which do you think I should do?"

This gets almost a 100% response rate, since you have actually done the work in advance...plus all the busy person has to do is tell you which option is best. GOOD JOB.

Ask Excellent Questions

I used to go into a meeting with my mentors and ask these really generic questions, "What are the top 3 things that made you successful?"

What a BS question! If I asked you that right now, what would you say? Probably something like, "I worked hard. I set my priorities..." What does this even mean? It doesn't mean anything, because I asked a bad question.

I like to write down my questions ahead of time, and then I imagine the answers. If I say, "What are three reasons you're successful?" People are going to give you really generic answers. "Oh, I have my priorities straight," etc. That doesn't help you at all!

Scratch that question. Instead I might say something like, "What surprised you about your business in the last year, where you doubled your revenue?"

What do I imagine their answers are going to be? They'll say something like, "You know, I knew that our product was excellent and it would sell. But what I didn't realize was that my relationships that I built 10 years ago would be critical for locking up so many big orders."

Is that interesting? Yes, I want to know more. So that's a question I'll ask. You see the point?

So many of us go into these meetings without having thought through our questions. Write them down the first few times and go through the process of answering them.

Is this actually an interesting question? Is the answer going to be interesting? If not, strike it. If yes, then it's earned its way onto the page.

Let the Relationship Take It's Course

My friend Ben Casnocha, who's been mentored by people like Reid Hoffman, the CEO of LinkedIn, told me, "Mentorship relationships happen naturally. The best ones aren't transactional. You're not keeping score. You want to reach out to someone and develop rapport. And over time, you can begin to see that person as a mentor."

I asked Ben how long would it realistically take to build this relationship.

Without missing a beat, he said, "4 to 5 years."

"And that's with having regular communication. It takes a long time, and it takes a lot of helpful communications with the person. You have to follow the natural pace."

My favorite way of starting up those regular communications and building rapport is taking people out to coffee. You have to reach out to potential mentors and ask them about them. They love being experts in what they're asked about—as long as you're asking good questions.

Take someone out to coffee, on their terms, at their convenience. I try to spend 50 minutes out of an hour, just asking them questions. Of course, you're asking questions because you're really trying to learn, not just for the sake of asking questions.

Maybe for the last 10 minutes I talk about myself a little bit, and set the tone for meeting them again. However, that first meeting is as little about me as possible. I want to learn from them.

Most importantly, don't rush it. Nothing damages this kind of relationship more than someone who is overanxious and becomes more of a pest than a person who's interested in a long-term, mutually beneficial relationship.

Find Ways to Give Value

Once a rapport has been built, it's time to think about how you can add value to the other person. Most people tend to freak out and over think this. "They're so much more successful than me! How am I supposed to add value to them?"

True, if you're at coffee with a Fortune 500 CEO, you're probably not going to add value with management strategies or your insights into their profit and loss statement.

But look at what Charlie Hoehn and Ryan Holiday did. One of Charlie's first assignments with Tim Ferriss was to book a theater for a special screening of a James Bond film for Tim's friends. This was added value because it saved Tim his most valuable resource: *time*.

Ryan added value to Tucker Max by finding interesting articles, then by trying to sell ad space. He tried to both save Tucker time, and earn him money.

One of the best ways I added value to CEOs was by giving presentations on how millennials used technology. Millennials were their target market but they had no idea how they spent their time: Were they watching TV? If so, on the television set or laptop or on their phone? How much time did they spend on television vs. Facebook? Why?

In 100 different topics, these CEOs had years of experience on me. So I focused on the one topic where I could contribute, and it was a HUGE value for them.

Build the Relationship Instead of Asking for it

Remember, when you're looking for a mentor, it's not about asking them, "Will you be my mentor?" That basically disqualifies you immediately. You're showing what a novice you are with this one question.

Instead, it's about showing what you can offer them, not asking for anything, and building a relationship. Over time you may find that you can pick up the phone and ask them your toughest questions, and you can get an answer that will save you months or even years of your life.

That's the power of attracting a mentor.

11. MENTAL TOUGHNESS: HOW TO MASTER SETBACKS, FAILURE, AND EVEN SUCCESS

I remember my trainer stacking on weights and saying, "OK, 10-10-10."

He meant 10 cleans, 10 push-ups, 10 pull-ups…times 10. I just shook my head and got started. On the 5th set, I had slowed way down. I was catching my breath when I heard the voice in my head, "I can't do any more. My heart is beating too fast. I should just sit down and rest."

I hate that voice. I hate it because every time I listen to it and quit, I regret it and want to go back in time and slap myself in the face. But it was getting louder and louder in my head.

Then something happened. As I was thinking about quitting, I saw my trainer add more weight for my next set. I was about to quit, and he was adding more weight!

He said, "COME ON!!" And I shook my head again, took a deep breath, and went for it.

I wasn't the fastest, but I finished. And as I walked out of there, I realized I'd learned more in that one training session than from reading 20 books about business:

I thought I couldn't go on, and I was getting ready to quit, but instead of letting me quit or even coast, my coach pushed me to do even more.

And I did it. This was a magical moment for me.

It made me think about how easy it is to quit—and how rare it is to find someone who'll push you harder than you even thought was possible.

Mark Divine, my friend and retired Navy Seal Commander, shared a similar experience. He was on the verge of Hell Week during SEAL training. Hell Week is generally considered the most arduous period of military training in any special-ops branch in the world.

His instructor said to him: "Don't worry about this. This is an easy day. You're capable of 20 times what you think you are."

They started on Sunday. "By Wednesday I was getting more alert," Mark said. "My body also started to get stronger. I actually started to develop muscle mass. So by Thursday of Hell Week I was developing muscle mass and I was starting to feel really strong, both physically, mentally, and emotionally."

What's any of this got to do with you growing your online business? Everything.

In every entrepreneur's journey, he or she will run into incredible resistance. Take a look:

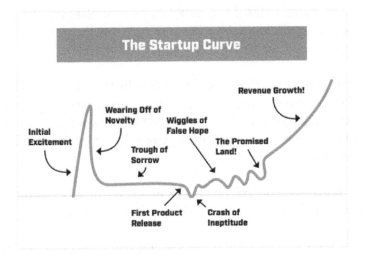

It's in the "Trough of Sorrow" where mental toughness becomes crucial. It's where many entrepreneurs give up, and let the short-term setback stop them from building a 6-figure business.

These moments are inevitable. Most entrepreneurs go through it in some form:

> *"One of the hardest things about failing from the get-go is I felt I had to hide it from my friends and family…It was a really hard time in my life."*—Bryce C.

> *"About two years ago, I decided that I wanted to try the online [business] thing. I actually left my full-time position at my company…That was really the first time where I experienced putting effort into something and then crossing my fingers and hoping for a result and seeing absolutely nothing. It's like you're used to succeeding your entire life and then all of a sudden, you'd come up against a brick wall."*—Tom M.

"I was afraid I'd have to move back home to Alabama. I kept asking myself, 'Am I doing this right? Am I making enough?' I was afraid I wouldn't be able to pay rent."—Sarah J.

The entrepreneur's journey is infected by the Facebook effect. Most business owners compare their day-to-day to everyone else's highlight reel. You go on Facebook, what do you see? "Oh, I love being on the beach. Costa Rica is so beautiful on a Wednesday!"

At home, you're like, "What? I'm sitting in here trying to launch this online business. What is going on here?"

The tools to weather the journey and stay mentally tough are just as important as your email newsletter tool or your email capture form, if not more so.

The Power of Unshakable Confidence

We all know that person. Someone who's got it all figured out...their business is taking off, they are amazing at their 9-5, AND never miss their kid's football games. You look at them and wonder, "How are you so confident? How do you have it all under control?"

I call this "unshakable confidence." How can we as entrepreneurs build it?

Imagine you wanted to build an online business similar to IWT. You look at what it'll take. First, you'll start a blog. Then you realize, "Oh, no, I have to get a domain. I have to register it, and then I have to set up an email list, and then I have to write every day. Wow, that's overwhelming."

It is overwhelming...yet to someone who's been doing it for years, it seems effortless. They wake up, write a blog post, and hit publish. Ten thousand people see it and 200 leave a comment. If we're starting out, how can we do the same?

What's the difference between the 2 people? One difference: Realizing that almost anything can be figured out. In fact, as my friend Marie Forleo says, "Everything is figure-out-able."

One person, who's not confident, sees all those challenges to starting an online business. Email list, domain, URL, writing all the time..."Ahhhh! Overwhelming! No, that's too much stuff. I can't do it."

The second person has to go through the exact same things, but their mindset is totally different. Instead of saying, "Oh, my God, that's overwhelming," they say, "Okay, what are all the things I possibly need to do?" They write them down, as many as they can.

Next, they look at their list. "Okay, each of these things is going to be valuable and it's going to be fun. I'm going to learn something new." Setting up an email list? No idea how to do it. What does it involve? What are the best vendors? How much does it cost? They start Googling. And instead of feeling overwhelmed, they think, "I'm going to learn how to set up an email list. Once I learn, I'll know it forever."

You repeat this process over and over again, for each item on your list. With each step, your confidence builds, slowly creating powerful, unshakable confidence.

How to Never Be Afraid of Failure

Failure is one of the big "F words" in our culture. I want to tweak the way that you think about failure, because I've failed a lot over the last few years. In fact, I fail so often, I have a failures folder set up in my email account. If I'm not sending five to seven failures there a month, I'm actually failing at failing. I know that I'm not trying enough, so I'm not failing enough, as well.

You can see just in that simple example how I think about failure totally differently than many people. Many of us believe, if we fail at something we're going to be marked with a scarlet letter forever. In fact, some of us have never experienced failure at all.

Think of something you're not particularly good at. For me, it's math. I was never really good at math. Yet, my businesses include online business and personal finance. I cover conversion strategy and becoming rich, and I do math on a daily basis. There are a few different options to get over the idea of failure and get on with your business.

First, actually get better. There's no way around this. It can be difficult or challenging to practice something over and over again, forcing yourself to get better. In my math example, that would mean reading math books, practicing problems, etc.

For running your business, it might be writing blog posts. Or staying on top of all the business administration. Or selling your goods or service. The unsexy but powerful thing is to just spend the time getting better at something you're not good at.

Second, reframe failure. Let's say that you're terrible at cardio. You hate running on the treadmill, like I do. I'd rather do pull-ups until my arms fell off than get on that treadmill. So what can I do?

I reframe failure. I say, "Okay, yesterday I ran for 7 minutes and I was exhausted. I felt like I was going to die. Today, I'm going to just try for 7 minutes and 30 seconds. If I run for that extra 30 seconds, it's undeniable that I'm getting better."

See how that's a reframe? Frankly, it's embarrassing for me to admit I can only run for 7 minutes, but I reframed it. By adding the 30 seconds, it becomes a growth trajectory.

Another powerful reframe my students use: "It's not a failure. It's a test." No one clicked on your email? Not a failure, you just tested that headline. No one bought on your sales page? That's a test of your offer, now you know you need to rethink the benefits of your product or service.

Third, prepare for failure. It's okay to think, "I'm probably going to fail at this, so let me prepare." I call this a failure expectation strategy, and it's helped in so many areas of my life. For example, I had a failure expectation strategy when I was applying to colleges. I expected to get rejected by a number of colleges, including Stanford, because it's a competitive school.

I planned out ahead of time, "What will I do if I get rejected?" In this case, I was going to send additional press clippings from the newspaper. I was going to send an update on my grades and a new essay I'd written. If I failed, it would have just been another stepping stone to eventual success.

In your business, the better your failure expectation strategy, the faster you'll grow. For example, let's say you sell a make-up tutorial course. You send it out to some friends and family who might be interested, but all you hear are crickets.

Fortunately, you have failure expectation strategies up your pocket. You tell another group of friends, but this time, you bundle your offer with a complimentary 30-minute Skype consultation, and this time, you get 2 buyers. Interesting...You sell to another group, and bundle it with your favorite bronzer set, and this time 10 people buy.

Suddenly, more orders are coming in, and you're in business, because you used your failure expectation strategy. We also call this "failing forward," because each failure propels your business another step ahead, until it's inevitable that you become successful.

A word of caution about failure: If you set really unrealistic goals, there is a cost to failure. If you say, "Okay, I'm feeling really motivated. I'm going to sit down and write an entire sales letter or write 7 emails pitching my product, which I've been putting off for the last 3 months. I'm going to buckle down and get it done..."

If you use generic phrases like "feeling motivated" and "I'm going to buckle down," I can tell you you're already going to fail. And after failing multiple times, you'll start to see yourself as a "person who fails." In other words, you start to believe, "I'm not the kind of person who can succeed in business."

If fear of failure is paralyzing you, then I strongly recommend you set a tiny, realistic goal for the day. When you achieve it, then move on to the next tiny, realistic goal. Your business is going to see better results from taking action on small goals then dreaming about unrealistic big goals that you never achieve.

Failure is a normal part of business. You don't have to be a weirdo and track all your failures like me, but if you don't have 3 things you've failed at in the last 6 months, you're probably not trying enough. A friend once gave me some great advice at a tricky time in my career.

She said: "Ramit, nobody cares what you did. They only care what you're doing."

This completely shifted the way I looked at failure, and is a reason for a lot of my success today.

Stop Worrying About Falling Behind

In my program *Zero to Launch*, students learn all the steps to build an online business. Inevitably, new students join, see how much progress other people have made, and they freak out.

Here's one email I got, where a student wrote: "I see many folks who seem to have been making progress within the course, and I not only feel left behind but confused as to where I might be missing something important."

The fact of the matter is, when it comes to this program, there are some superstar students, but they're probably only about 5% of the student population. They just happen to post frequently, and so you see their results.

It can get uncomfortable after a while, I get that. How did they get 2,000 people to sign up for their newsletter this week?

How did they just make $15,000 in sales this month? What am I missing?

I get that. I'm in communities, too, where it's like, "What am I doing wrong? Did I miss a certain slide in the program, and everyone else got it except for me?"

The truth is, this is supposed to be hard.

But if you compare yourself to what everyone else is doing, you're going to be stuck there forever for no reason at all.

A while back I posted a short video of me bowling. Like any person who grew up in suburbia, I am the man at bowling. I go up, I look at the camera, and I said, "Here we go." Boom! Knock them all down! Fist bump!

If you watched it, you'd probably think, "Okay, this guy is pretty good."

Except no one saw the other video we shot...Same cameraperson, similar set-up. I look at the camera, approach the lane, and completely EAT IT. I slip and fall down. The people next to me are laughing, the camera is shaking because the person is laughing.

Interestingly, that one didn't make it to social media. So if you had just looked at my feed, it just looks like I'm great at bowling.

The fact is, that was just one success I happened to capture on camera, and the same thing is true when comparing your business to someone else's. You might see someone who launched a $10,000 product. Amazing, good for them, and I want them to succeed even more. But what we don't see are all the mistakes they made, all the misses, all the times they fell down. They're there, trust me, they just don't want you to see them.

Here's a simple technique that allowed me to eliminate 99% of these worries about what how others are doing. It goes like this:

Focus on what you can control, ignore what you cannot.

That sounds obvious, but when we look at our actual behavior, it's actually quite unbelievable how much time we spend focusing on the things we cannot control. For example, the economy, politics, negative people, other people's businesses, these are all things we generally cannot control, and yet we spend a lot of energy worrying about them.

Once I was getting ready for a TV spot. I was getting my makeup done, and the makeup lady gets really angry with me. She said, "So you're this finance guy, huh? You know they just started taking $200.00 a week out of my paycheck."

"Who's they?" I ask.

"You know, the government."

I remember thinking to myself, "I don't think the government is suddenly taking $10,000.00 a year out of her paycheck." But she was convinced. She was convinced that the government suddenly decided to take $10,000 a year from her.

"What should I do about it?"

I smiled. "You know you could certainly look into that. You should try to find out exactly who's taking this money out of your paycheck. But, let me ask you a question. Do you have a 401K?"

"Yes," she said.

"Have you maxed it out?"

"I don't know."

"What about a Roth IRA?" I asked. "Do you know what that is?"

"Yeah. I have one. I didn't put anything in this year. Last year I contributed a little bit..." And at that moment, she kind of got the point, which is it's easy to complain about what "the government" is doing, or how bad the economy is.

Yet the things in front of her, the very things she has control over, she was not doing.

Why is that? Because we hear from all the media around us how bad things are, and it actually feels great to be able to complain about it and stick it to somebody and tell them, "I can't believe this!"

What we want to focus on is improving ourselves. Remember, building a business is supposed to be challenging, otherwise everyone else would do it. So I just focus on what I can control, and ignore everything else.

For example, when I see someone who's super successful, I don't let myself get jealous. I force myself to reframe the situation. I'll say to myself, "That's great, I'm happy for them. We're all at different stages. What could I learn from what they did?" If I can, I'll even message them or shoot them an email.

I'd say, "That is amazing. Can you tell me what part of the process helped you the most? How did you focus on your copywriting because I noticed that it's really vibrant?"

This is how we become amazing entrepreneurs. We develop the skills to become mentally tough, to push through the trough of sorrow that EVERY business owner goes through. Then we look at the other entrepreneurs around us and use them for support. We ask for help. We ask excellent questions. And together, we all grow.

12. FIELD REPORT: 44% GROWTH WITHOUT ANY NEW PRODUCTS BY GRAHAM COCHRANE

Graham Cochrane is an audio engineer who helps musicians create professional-sounding mixes using home studio gear. He grew his business from $250,000 to $600,000 a year.

Why do so many business owners turn to flash sales, a rotating door of new products, and spending gobs of money on Facebook ads to increase revenue, when there are other growth strategies that involve much less work, cost nothing, and don't cheapen your brand?

Just over 18 months ago, I increased my monthly income by more than 44% without launching a new product or service, or doing any advertising of any kind.

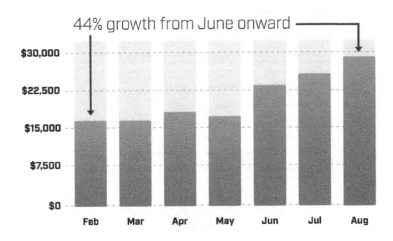

My average monthly sales through May 2014 were $16,739. By August, that shot up to $24,609.

Instead, I made three simple, yet profoundly powerful tweaks to my business that you can implement in a weekend. Over time, you will see great results pile up as well.

I want to walk you through all three.

Put the Spotlight on your Reader

At its core, every business involves a simple transaction. Money changes hands as a product or service is delivered.

In my case, my products are online courses that teach people how to record and mix really good sounding music in their affordable bedroom studios. I sell information. Plain and simple. That being said, many of my early sales pages were just that—both plain and simple in their communication.

Take a look at one of my old sales pages.

Want Better Sounding Vocals?

We all want to produce top notch vocals in our recordings. Whether we're tracking our own songs at home or producing vocals for paid clients, we know that a polished vocal can make or break a recording.

But capturing a great vocal is more than just buying a great mic and letting the singer rip. There are some key behind-the-scenes steps that take place in order to create that crystal clear, punchy, and vibrant vocal we all hear on the radio

Can you identify with any of these statements?

→ My vocals sound lifeless and boring.

→ I can't seem to get vocalists to deliver a great take in the studio.

→ I hate editing vocals because I can always "hear" my edits.

→ Pitch correction just scares me...I either over do it, or don't do it right.

→ Compared to my backing tracks, my vocals sound amateur. Like they were obviously recorded at home.

Lack of expensive gear is probably not your problem! You need a better workflow and some guidance...

Enter REthink Vocals

REthink Vocals is an in depth, simple to understand, and easy to implement video series that can help you

Within just a few lines I'm already talking about the product and why it's so great.

(Note: If the images in this chapter are difficult to read, don't worry. You can find better quality ones linked on our bonus site: growthlab.com/your-move.)

There was nothing inherently bad or wrong about these sales pages. They clearly stated what the course was about, who it was for, and why it was a smart purchase. And of course it stated the price, and included a big "Buy Now" button.

And the great thing—these sales pages made me money.

Sales had been coming in month after month on pages like this for about 4 years. I was earning a very good living. There's nothing tricky about business; you simply need to offer tremendous value to people and solve one of their challenges or frustrations. My courses were doing just that.

But by simply changing the words you use to sell your products, you can drastically increase revenue. Learning a lot about the psychology of words from guys like Ramit Sethi, I decided to try my hand at rewriting the sales copy for my three most popular courses. And this time instead of simply conveying information about the product, I decided to put the spotlight on the potential customer.

This is key. I spent way more time (i.e. wrote more words) at the beginning of the sales page focusing on the reader and identifying their biggest pains, challenges, and frustrations as they relate to my niche. I also articulated their biggest hopes, dreams, and goals related to the topic of recording music.

Take a look at one of my newer sales pages.

Notice how much time I take to articulate the pain point here.

This immediately draws them in as they say, "Yes! This guy gets me!" Because don't we all like talking to people who understand us at a deep level? Don't we trust them more?

While many of my competitors use their words to harp on how many hours of HD video their courses include, and how much extra "stuff" you get when you purchase, I instead use my words to focus on the customer. What do they want? What are they frustrated with? What is going on inside their heads?

By spending more of your sales pages connecting with the potential customer at this deep level, you create the trust and credibility that makes him want to keep reading to discover your "solution" to his problem.

And because you understand his problem and make sure he knows it, when you offer your product (the solution), he cares little about the features, what's included, or even the price for that matter. All he cares about is the solution that you can offer him.

To do this with your current lineup of products or services, try this: Send out an email to your mailing list, or reach out to your fans or followers on social media and ask them two questions:

- What is your biggest frustration or challenge [related to your niche] right now?
- What are your biggest hopes and dreams [related to your niche] this coming year?

The answers you get will be worth thousands of dollars to you as you gain deeper insight into the minds of your customers.

Offer Supersized Options

One of the most classic techniques for increasing sales is also the simplest: upsells.

If you've ever been to McDonald's and ordered a hamburger, then you've witnessed quite possibly the most profitable upsell ever: "Do you want fries with that?" Another variation is when you order a combo meal and they ask you, "Do you want to supersize that?"

Some people will answer "No" to both of those questions. No harm done. But many people will say, "Yes." Instant increase in sales.

You see, at McDonald's, people have already been convinced they want the product. They are prepared to part with their money and they know what they are getting. In this moment they are in a buying mood.

At the point of sale, employees have been trained to offer the customer something more as an option. The customer wasn't planning on spending more, but because it's a desirable upsell and they are about to part with their money anyway, it's a no-pressure situation with pretty high conversion rates.

If you pay attention, you'll see upsells everywhere you go.

Oddly enough, I was very aware of upselling as a business strategy, yet I wasn't doing it in my own business. For years I simply offered each of my products in one version. One price. One option. One size fits all.

Big mistake.

I finally got smart and decided that it couldn't hurt to offer one or two more expensive versions of my courses and leave it for my customers to decide which was a good fit for them.

Take a look at one of my most popular courses, REthink Mixing. I had been selling this course at its original price of $99 for three years.

I still offer it at $99, but now I've added two other versions: one that costs $149 and includes bonus content and a custom mix critique from me (where I'll actually listen to one of their songs and give them email feedback), and one that costs $349 and includes everything from the lower tiers plus a one-hour Skype call with me.

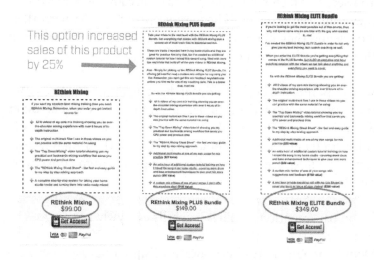

If one person purchases the upper tier, it's almost like 4 people buying the original course!

Few people go for the $349 version (although I sell some every month), but the cool thing is that roughly half of my customers go for the middle tier at $149. That means that I can still sell a $99 course that I made years ago, but now I can get a 25% boost in revenue from it (50% of the customers spending 50% more).

I've applied this upselling, supersized concept to just about all of my courses now, and it works great. You can easily do it, too.

What is your most popular product or service? Can you add a slightly more expensive version of it? What ways could you add more value to it that don't take too much money or effort, but still allow you to charge 50-100% more for it?

One final thought: When you give people a choice of product or service tiers, you do something subtle but powerful. You shift the internal question for the customer from, "Should I buy this?" to "Which one should I buy?"

That one simple mental shift is so profound, as it gets them thinking which one is a better fit. This moves them beyond whether the product as a whole is a good fit, and it can do wonders for your sales conversion, even if they go with the lower tier.

Sell Sooner (and More Often)

My business is built around free content. I write articles and make videos that can help people make better sounding recordings—and 95% of this training is free.

That is how you start the relationship with future customers: Offer them something valuable first. This allows them to see if you can deliver what they want and need, and if you are trustworthy. It's such a huge part of what I do and I love it.

But we're still running businesses. I have a lovely wife and two beautiful daughters to feed, clothe, and provide shelter for, so I need to make money somehow. And the same is true with you—you're reading this because you want to not only help people, but also make money!

That's where my in-depth video courses come into the picture.

In the past, I was a bit scared to sell them. Not because they weren't any good, but because I was afraid of turning people off by asking for a sale so soon in the relationship.

I sell via email. I encourage readers and viewers who enjoy my free stuff to join my email list where they can get even more incredible free resources that I don't offer anywhere else. Once they join that list, they are sent a series of pre-written emails over the course of a few weeks.

Before these tweaks, most of my emails contained more free bonus information and resources. This went on for at least two weeks, when eventually they would get an email that mentioned one of my paid courses. Then the cycle repeated.

The paid course was almost apologetically included in an email as if I were saying, "Sorry to bother you, but I have these other courses that aren't free, but I think you might like them, but if you don't it's OK, I'll send you more free stuff, too!"

Just like my plain and simple sales pages, this email campaign worked. I still made sales.

But you can make even more sales by simply changing two things: how early on you offer your paid products, and how often you offer them.

I've heard wildly different philosophies on this. Some say you should sell as soon as possible. Others say you need to establish a relationship for weeks and weeks before offering your audience something to buy.

I was fed up with my scaredy-cat approach to selling and wanted to try a more confident model.

What helped shift my mindset is something Jay Abraham calls being your client or customer's "trusted advisor." If you view yourself as their trusted advisor, and you have a product or service that will truly help them, then you should be doing everything in your power to let them know about it and offer it to them.

This concept blew me away. Stop and ask yourself: Are your products awesome? Do they really help people? If the answer is "No," then you need to make a better product.

Fortunately for me, my answer was, "Yes. My online courses are the best out there. They've helped thousands of people and they can help thousands more."

With that confidence in hand, I decided to delete all of my auto-responder emails (the pre-written emails I mentioned before) and start over fresh. This time I made sure that 3 days in, I was offering one of my products. And not just with one email, but with 3 consecutive emails.

I still delivered value first (and after), but I made sure that my email campaign moved quickly into offering the best thing for them—my paid products.

Now, over the course of 60 days, my email subscribers not only get tons of free resources and exclusive training, but they get offered 5 products for a total of 3 times each. This means they are getting offered my best stuff 15 times in the first two months.

This totally changed my sales revenue. I sell more courses, help more people, and make more money. And the best part? It doesn't cost a thing, and is happening on autopilot each and every day.

What would happen if you started to offer your best stuff to potential clients/customers sooner and more often than you currently do?

Sure, some people would say "No." And maybe a few people would be irritated. But remember, if you are their trusted advisor, and your product or service truly is world-class and can make their lives better, then offering it to them sooner and more often is the best thing for them!

Want a 30% Raise This Year?
Consider this...

What if you changed the words on all your sales and promotional material, taking the focus off of your product or service and shifting it onto your potential customers? Maybe you boost sales by 10%.

And what if you offered a more expensive option to your core product or service costing about 50% more? If only a quarter of your customers go for the upper tier, you'll have a 12.5% increase in revenue.

Finally, what if you began selling to your prospective clients sooner and more often, always reminding them that your product or service truly can solve their problems and help them realize their dreams and hopes? Just by simply asking for the sale twice as much as you currently do, you'll likely get at least a 10% boost in revenue.

Add all three tweaks up, and you're looking at more than a 30% increase in revenue in the next 12 months. Maybe even immediately. And those are pretty conservative numbers.

What could that do for your life with a 30% raise this year?

NOW IT'S YOUR TURN

Thanks for reading this book.

You've unpacked the core lessons my students and I spent over 10 years testing, tweaking, and curating. These are the exact lessons that have helped us launch thousands of businesses and generate revenue that's allowed people to quit their 9-5s, travel the world, or just spend more time with their families.

In other words, you've learned the core lessons to starting, running, and growing your business—and putting you back in the driver's seat of your life.

I'd like for you to do 2 things now:

1. Come on by to growthlab.com/your-move so I can send you several pieces of unreleased material.
2. Tell a friend. Every one of your friends could benefit from at least one page in this book. Share it with them, send them a link—whatever it takes. I'd appreciate it.

Thanks,

Ramit Sethi

CEO, *I Will Teach You To Be Rich*

ABOUT RAMIT SETHI

Ramit Sethi is a *New York Times bestselling author*, founder of PBWiki—a venture-backed tech startup—and CEO of *I Will Teach You To Be Rich* and *Growth Lab*.

Over the past decade, Sethi has grown his dorm room blog into a multi-million dollar company, with more than 30,000 paying customers.

His work has been featured in Entrepreneur Magazine, CNN, Forbes, Fortune, the New York Times, 99U, and more.

To learn more about Ramit, please go to iwillteachyoutoberich.com or growthlab.com.

Or you can look for his previous *New York Times* bestseller **_I Will Teach You To Be Rich_** wherever books are sold.

ABOUT GROWTHLAB

GrowthLab is our online publication that delivers battle-tested insights for starting and growing your online business.

Each week we feature no-BS strategies and tactics from top entrepreneurs to help you drive results and build the business (and life) you want. Subscribe today at GrowthLab.com.

Our Products

Zero to Launch: **Start and grow your own online business**.

Call to Action: **Double your conversions**.

Accelerator: **Get advanced business coaching**.

Made in United States
Orlando, FL
03 October 2024